HENRY HARRISSE ON COLLEGIATE EDUCATION

Henry Harrisse is known for his distinguished work as bibliographer, as energetic student of the literature of the discovery of the New World, and for his contributions to the literature of history and geography. From the little that has been written on or about this man and his life of "tumultuous scholarship" and from some of his own writings he appears as a very individualistic and somewhat erratic character. But very important in the long list of his writings are two essays on collegiate education, apparently written when he was at the University of North Carolina in the 1850's. One of these was published at Columbia, South Carolina, in 1857. The other essay, apparently never until now published, is given below and contains also views on collegiate education which may have some interest and significance for higher educational institutions in this country today.

It is believed that Harrisse was born in France in the second quarter of the nineteenth century, although there are conflicting statements about the exact place and date of his birth.[1] His first appearance in this country is said to have been in Charleston, South Carolina, when he was perhaps about eighteen years of age. It is also said that he had a post as teacher in Mount Zion Academy at Winnsboro in that state; and it is suggested that his keen intellectual qualities were highly respected by President James H. Thornwell (he refers to him as "the eminent Dr. Thornwell"), of the South Carolina College, which in 1853 conferred on Harrisse an honorary master's degree.[2] Harrisse

---

[1] Kemp P. Battle refers to him as "A native Frenchman" and spells the name Herrissee. *History of the University of North Carolina,* I, 644. See Randolph G. Adams, *Three Americanists* (Philadelphia: University of Pennsylvania Press, 1939). Michael Kraus, in *A History of American History,* p. 294, says "Harrisse was born in Paris in 1830, came to the United States as a child, and studied at the University of South Carolina." See Henry Vignaud, *Henry Harrisse, Etude Biographique et Morale.* (Paris: 1912). Vignaud says (page 5) that Harrisse "cachait le lieu et la date de sa naissance." He suggests that perhaps Harrisse feared that if people knew from whence he came they would know what he wished to conceal; that he was weak enough to hide the fact that the blue blood of the Ayrans did not flow fully in his veins and "qu'il appartenait à la grande famille sémitique." Vignaud also says that Harrisse was the son of a furrier who was believed to have come from Russia and, although an Israelite, married a Parisian, and that Harrisse was born in Paris March 23, 1829. See also *The National Cyclopaedia of American Biography,* XVIII, 37, 38.

[2] Adams, *Three Americanists,* p. 1. The *Catalogue of South Carolina College for 1854,* p. 29, lists Harrisse as one of those "persons upon whom honorary degrees have been conferred besides those that are included amongst the bachelor of arts-year, 1853-degree, A.M." The citation is not given. Letter of July 8, 1946, to Edgar W. Knight from Ruth Jones, Assistant to the Director of The South Caroliniana Library, University of South Carolina. Afterwards Harrisse generally followed his name to most of his letters with "A.M." But opposite page 4 of his autobiographic letter to Barlow, in which he included the title page of his translation of the philosophical works of Descartes, he wrote "Henry Harrisse A.M. [*sic!*]."

[1]

seems to have been acquainted with and had high respect for Thornwell's educational views which students of American educational history consider sound and highly advanced for the time. There is some internal evidence that Harrisse was acquainted with *Thoughts on the Present Collegiate System in the United States,* by President Francis Wayland of Brown University, which was published in Boston in 1842 and is accounted one of the distinguished discussions of the subject before 1860; and also with the energetic interest of Professor George Ticknor of Harvard College in improving collegiate education in that institution and perhaps in the United States generally.[3]

Harrissee became an instructor in French in the University of North Carolina in 1853 and later was "professor *pro tem* in the Georgetown Jesuit's College" in Washington. He became a lawyer and said that he had gone to Chapel Hill to study law. He sought the advice of Judah P. Benjamin on opportunities for legal practice in New Orleans but, influenced by Stephen A. Douglas's "all sorts of promises of preferment," went to Chicago instead and there in September, 1857, Harrisse set himself up as a lawyer. Apparently somewhat an indifferent practitioner of the law, he dabbled a bit in journalism in that city until a lucky coincidence took him in the early 1860's to New York and a post as "legal correspondent to the Havana branch of a Spanish bank." In that city he met and made a fast friendship with Samuel L. M. Barlow, influential and successful lawyer, connoisseur of art, and enthusiastic book-collector, especially of rare items of Americana. In these artistic and literary interests Harrisse was very much at home; and two decades later he wrote for Barlow some confidential autobiographic sketches or letters which provide some information concerning Harrisse's extraordinary career.[4] "Yes, twenty years have now elapsed

---

[3] Ticknor wrote to Thomas Jefferson, June 16, 1823, and tried to arouse the interest of the father of the University of Virginia in higher educational reform. Jefferson's reply, July 16 of that year, furnishes one of his earliest explicit statements on the elective system. In that reply he said: "I am not fully informed of the practices at Harvard, but there is one from which we shall certainly vary, although it has been copied, I believe, by nearly every college and academy in the United States. That is, the holding the students all to one prescribed course of reading, and disallowing exclusive application to those branches only which are to qualify them for the particular vocations to which they are destined. We shall, on the contrary, allow them uncontrolled choice in the lectures they shall choose to attend, and require elementary qualification only, and sufficient age. . . . The rock which I most dread is the discipline of the institution, and it is that on which most of our public schools labor. The insubordination of our youth is now the greatest obstacle in their education." H. A. Washington (editor), *The Writings of Thomas Jefferson,* VII, 300-302.
[4] Adams, *Three Americanists,* pp. 6-8. These materials, by Harrisse's request never published, are in the New York Public Library. A photocopy is in the University of North Carolina library, Chapel Hill.

since I first ventured to knock at your door on Fifth Avenue, begging leave to examine. . . ." Harrisse was always examining, with or perhaps without leave, in an effort to get at the sources of things historical.

Harrisse is perhaps best and most favorably known for his services to American scholarship. He was a keen student, a bibliophile and devoted book-collector, a distinguished bibliographer, the author of the "monumental volume," *Bibliotheca Americana Vetustissima*, and remarkable works on Columbus, and he "produced no less than ninety-one separate titles, books, monographs, papers and articles, each one of which was a noteworthy contribution to American history." [5] Harrisse is also known for his unhappy experiences at Chapel Hill with students, colleagues, the administration, and the trustees.[6] In the University of North Carolina he "raised the devil generally on the board of trustees and faculty of her University by my strenuous efforts to improve the curriculum and pedagogical methods according to a system of my own." [7]

In a volume in the New York Public Library entitled "Essays, Memorials, etc., 1854-1857 Harrisse," appears a letter of October 23, 1856, written by Harrisse from Chapel Hill to the "Executive Committee of the Board of Trustees" of the University of North Carolina, Raleigh, which shows that he and the authorities of that institution must have got along badly together:

Gentlemen:
In writing the sundry memorials which were lately laid before the Board, my object was to promote the best interests of the University. To that end I have pointed out the reforms which were needed, and adduced all the necessary proofs. I can do no more!
Very much against my wishes, and contrary to my expectations, the contest is degenerating into a personal strife; which can only injure the future welfare of the institution.

---
[5] Adams, *Three Americanists*, p. 2.
[6] Harrisse was sharply critical of trustees, as will be seen from his discussion of that subject in the essay below.
[7] Harrisse to Barlow, autobiographic letter, p. 35. The date of the letter is August 10, 1883. In his letter accompanying the autobiographic materials Harrisse called them "the rigmarole I wrote against time and to kill it. . . .
"Recollect that the accompanying *Epistola* is not to be printed,—at least in my life-time, if ever.
"The reasons are obvious. Its contents cannot afford the slightest interest to any one beyond two or three personal friends; and the style is a sort of gibberish, written 'with a running pen,,' which without considerable emendations would appear ridiculous in print." Harrisse also asked "that no one be allowed to take a copy" of the materials and only four "amiable persons," whom he named, were to be permitted to read them.

I am one of the youngest members of the faculty, and can be easily spared. Under such circumstances, I deem it proper to proffer my resignation of the office I hold in the University, to take effect at any time you may wish to appoint between today and the end of the present session.

Should the Committee decide to institute an inquiry, I ask leave to remain until it is carried out.

I have the honor to be, Gentlemen,
                 Your obedient servant
                 Henri Harrisse, A.M.
                 Instructor of French in the N. C. University.

The next page in the volume in the New York Public Library contains the following:

The Trustees decided in my favor against the faculty. Having thus attained my object, I returned my resignation, which was accepted the following session.

I had in the meanwhile graduated in the law school, and soon afterwards left the d——d place, never to see it again!
                 Hy H sse.
The University has since been squelched by Gov. Holden.[8]

This article deals, however, with Harrisse's interest in collegiate education, on which he published in 1857 *An Essay on the Literary Institution Best Adapted to the Present Wants and Interests of Our Country*.[9] This seems to have been an adaptation of "An Essay 'on the organization, regulation and management of a Literary Institution best adapted to the wants and interests of North Carolina'" which he had written in August,

---

[8] Although there is no date on this piquant comment, it was obviously written after Harrisse's letter of October 23, 1856. W. W. Holden was appointed provisional governor of North Carolina by President Johnson early in 1865 and served until December 15, 1865, and three years later he was elected governor of the state. Holden was a powerful member of the Board of Trustees of the University which at its first meeting under the new constitution of 1868 dismissed President David L. Swain and the faculty.
The letter above was written in connection with the "Hedrick case." Professor Benjamin Hedrick, native North Carolinian and an honor graduate of the University in the class of 1851, had been dismissed and his professorship declared vacant by the trustees October 18, 1856. He had always been a Democrat and in the state elections in August prior to his dismissal had voted the Democratic ticket, but he had expressed favor for John C. Fremont for the presidency of the United States on the newly formed Republican Party. Harrisse was the only member of the faculty who stood up for Hedrick during the unfortunate controversy. See J. G. deR. Hamilton, "Benjamin Sherwood Hedrick," *The James Sprunt Historical Publications*, Vol. 10, No. 1 (1910); R. D. W. Connor, *North Carolina*, II, 120-23; John Spencer Bassett, *Anti-Slavery Leaders in North Carolina*, pp. 29-47; Kemp P. Battle, *History of the University of North Carolina*, I, 524, 644, 655-57. Holden was editor of the *North Carolina Standard*, the most influential paper in the State, was the leader of the pro-slavery and secession sentiment in North Carolina, and was determined to drive Hedrick from Chapel Hill.
[9] Columbia, S. C.: Steam Power-Press of R. W. Gibbes, 1857. Adams, *Three Americanists*, p. 6, note 18, gives 1858 as the date of publication. The only copy of this essay that I have seen is in the New York Public Library and bears the date of 1857. A photocopy and a microcopy of the essay are in the University of North Carolina library, Chapel Hill.

1854.[10] In his autobiographic letter to Barlow, August 10, 1883 (note opposite page 35), Harrisse said that the essay written for the trustees of Normal College was "embodied in an *Essay on the Literary institution best adapted to the wants and interests of our own country*, printed at the expense of the Honb. William C. Preston, of South Carolina." In the same note Harrisse wrote that Barlow would find a copy of the North Carolina essay "in a MS. volume (4° size) containing my scrimmage with the Faculty, which I placed in the lower shelf of the book case on your right hand side when you face the window, *in the little room adjoining the black* library, about two feet from the corner. Next to it is a bound volume containing a series of N. C. University catalogues and addresses:— both of which I gladly make you a present of. But I don't want them to go with yr. library should you ever sell it."

The essay on a literary institution best suited to North Carolina led Harrisse into another kind of controversy which until now seems to have received no attention in the educational history of that state. This controversy had its origin in the early part of 1854 when the trustees of Normal College offered a prize of $200 for the best essay on the "Literary Institution" most suitable to that state. The announcement was as follows: [11]

A PRIZE ESSAY

The Trustees of Normal College will give $200 for the best essay on the organization, regulation and management of a Literary Institution best adapted to the wants and interests of North Carolina. The essay must determine the grade of the institution, whether College, Academy, High School, &c., the number, qualifications and duties of the trustees; the rules and regulations for teachers and students; the amount and method of instruction; expenses and building accommodations; whether students should study in private or classroom; whether they should board at private houses or at a steward's hall; whether the Institution should be denominational or otherwise, and all other things necessary to be known and determined in establishing and conducting an Institution.

---

[10] So far as I know this essay has never before been published. The original is the property of The New York Public Library and is used here by special permission. Letter from Robert W. Hill, Keeper of Manuscripts, to Edgar W. Knight, October 14, 1946.
[11] *Greensboro Patriot*, February 4, 1854. Normal College grew out of Union Institute and was given a charter by the legislature of North Carolina in 1851. This was amended November 21, 1852, and made the governor of North Carolina *ex officio* president and "the common school superintendent, should such an officer exist," ex officio secretary of the board of trustees of the institution. The office of state superintendent of common schools was created by legislative act, December 4, 1852, and Calvin H. Wiley assumed its duties, January, 1853.

Each competitor for the prize will direct his essay in a sealed envelope, postpaid, to B. Craven, Normal College, N. C., on or before the first day of September, 1854. The names of the judges will be published at least a month previous, said judges to be men of unquestioned ability. The trustees will retain for their own use, all essays examined, and pay the prize for the one selected by the judges.
Jan. 27, 1854.[12]

The materials which follow bear upon the competition for the prize of $200 in which Harrisse submitted his essay. But these materials do not indicate why the plans for the contest were not concluded; how many essays were submitted; why the writer of the letter of August, 1854, to President Craven (whether Harrisse or one of his friends) felt compelled to conceal his identity; nor the identity of the writer of the obviously satiric "Extracts from the Diary of a Diplomat." Adequate evidence on these questions seems now not to be accessible. But it is evident from the letters and other materials that follow that there was some disappointment — perhaps a bit of bitterness, on the part of Harrisse at least — and that the plans announced by President Craven, January 27, 1854, and published in the *Greensboro Patriot* the following February 4 were not carried through to fulfillment. In some of these materials appears suggestion of bad faith. Senator Reid wrote that if he had the power to do so he would have the matter "investigated with a view to having justice awarded to the competitors for the prize." A letter from a gentleman "of highest respectability" on the communication from Charleston, South Carolina, discussed in the *Greensboro Patriot* of March 3, 1855, said "there is apparently a breach of faith on the part of the Trustees of Normal College. . . ." And the editor of that paper in the same article expressed the hope that "some friend of Normal College will see the propriety of having the matter explained. . . ." Governor Thomas Bragg wrote on the subject at least once to President Craven and at least twice to Professor F. M. Hubbard, a colleague of Harrisse;

---

[12] A note on the page preceding the essay by Harrisse, in the volume in the New York Public Library, is as follows:
"The Essay by Henry Harrisse (for the $200 prize offered by the Trustees of the State Normal College) on the management of a Literary Institution best adapted to the wants and interest of North Carolina: with various Letters and other MS. relative to the non-fulfillment of the project by the Trustees, and the newspaper comments of that time, 1855.
"This collection includes two essays by Henri Harrisse, one printed, the other the original MS. with a key; the original letters of Gov. Thos. Bragg, the Hon. David S. Reid, B. Craven; the memorial of Henry Harrisse to the Board of Trustees; newspaper cuttings in reference to the Controversy which resulted in the dismissal of 'Mr. Black Republican Hedrick &&'[.]"

President Craven wrote to Professor Hedrick, also of the faculty of the University of North Carolina. Governor Bragg said in his letter to Professor Hubbard, May 4, 1855, that President Craven seemed "indignant that any one should suppose that he would permit a copy [of Harrisse's essay] to be taken." And Governor Bragg expressed the hope for an early end of the unfortunate matter.[13]

The controversy which these materials exhibit may seem after nearly a century a sort of *mons laborat, nascitur mus;* but for those immediately concerned in North Carolina in the middle 1850's it must have been more than a trivial episode. The contest doubtless provided some lively academic gossip in Chapel Hill.

As already noted, this article deals primarily with Harrisse's views on higher education a century ago. But out of the plans for the "prize essay" came not only the controversy here briefly treated but also the unpublished essay which follows and around which Harrisse evidently prepared the essay published at Columbia, South Carolina, in 1857. The earliest comment on the entire matter seems to be the following anonymous letter:

August 1854.

Mr. B. Craven
Normal College, N. C.

Dear Sir:
Sometime since I read in a stray paper,– the "Ballot Box" I believe– a notice said to have been originally published in the "Greensboro Patriot" by the Trustees of "Normal College" offering a prize of $200, for the "best essay on the organization, regulation and management of a Literary Institution best adapted to the wants and interest of North Carolina."

Having given some attention to the subject of collegiate institutions; trusting to the sincerity of the above proposal; and, being anxious to promote the cause of education within the range of my limited abilities, I immediately sat down to writing; and, now Sir, I take the liberty of requesting you to file the accompanying essay; or, submit

---

[13] The originals of the unsigned letter of August, 1854, to President Craven, "Extracts from the Diary of a Diplomat," the letter of Senator Reid to Harrisse, the letters of Governor Bragg to Professor Hubbard, and President Craven's letter to Professor Hedrick are in the New York Public Library. The items from the *Greensboro Patriot* may be found in the issues indicated. Clippings of these items are in the New York Public Library; photocopies and microcopies of all these materials now are in the library of the University of North Carolina, Chapel Hill. The letter from Harrisse to Reid, February 3, 1855, is in the State Department of Archives and History, Raleigh, and a photocopy is in the library of the University of North Carolina, Chapel Hill.

the same to the impartial consideration of the judges appointed to that effect.

Circumstances which I ought not to disclose, require me to conceal my name and place of residence. I shall, however, make myself known at no very distant time.

With sincere regards and deep regrets,
I am truly yours.

P.S. Being under the impression that this letter and its contents may never reach Randolph County, allow me to ask you to send a few lines directed to "X.Y.Z.4" *Baltimore Maryland*, stating whether you have received it.

If you desire to communicate anything else to me, you can do so, either through the same channel, or an insertion in the Greensboro Patriot of September 9*th* inst.

Yours &c &c

The next item on the controversy seems to be the following:

Columbia, S. C. Oct. 20th 1854.
Extracts from the Diary of a Diplomat.

Mr. Craven, I believe, (Mr. C. bows)— my name is Johnson, Sir, of So Carolina— would like if you are at leisure to have a few minutes conversation with you.— The object of my visit, Sir, is to obtain some information from you relative to an advertisement which appeared some months ago calling for essays on education in N Carolina— I represent a third party in the matter and am anxious to obtain for him all the facts of the case as it now stands.

Mr. C— They are soon told, Sir. We have had some unexpected detention in awarding the prize, but there will be no breach of faith. The chief difficulty was to find the right sort of men for judges; men who were bold enough to face something new and would yet have weight with the old system advocates. We expect to make up the number of judges this winter in Raleigh and the prizes will be certainly awarded before spring. (Dead pause)—

I suppose (said I) it will occupy them some time, the examination of the essays— you have received a good many I expect.

Yes, Sir, several. There have been 3 or 4 small affairs and two large ones, and now that the time has been extended I am expecting others daily; indeed I have been told I might expect some.

Well, what is the arrangement you intend to make, Mr. Craven, about the names of the authors— how will you identify the successful candidate?

Well, I suppose the writers will hand in their names in time in some sealed form or whatever plan they may select. As yet not one of them has given me his name.

Well, sir, what seems to be the favorite plan adopted by them— do they sign the piece with some fictitious name, or how?

No, Sir,— one of the large essays came without any sign or name attached— it was mailed from Baltimore and was accompanied by a letter (sealed) to the Examining Committee which of course I could not open. The other large one had no post mark at all upon it; but with directions that I should acknowledge the receipt by writing to— Armstrong, or XYZ Baltimore, which I directed the Post Master to do, and he told me he had done it. (q:e:d)

You still contemplate publishing the names of the judges, Mr. Craven, before the prize is awarded?

Oh yes, Sir. We thought that would be proper to have the names of the judges announced at least a month before the decision, in order to afford the candidates time to withdraw their essays in case they disliked the character of the judges.

(After a pause)— I rejoined "My friend was at a loss to explain the silence in the papers on the subject of the decision— so much time had elapsed since the day fixed for the essays to be all handed in, and—"

Yes, I suppose so, and I ought to have given some notice before now. As it is, I sent off only a few days ago a notice to be inserted in the Greensboro Patriot of next week, giving the description of the different modes adopted by each writer to introduce his piece to the Trustees, such as the directions he gave where to be addressed &c in order to let each know his piece had been received.

(Another pause)— I have your authority then for stating that other contributions will be yet received?

Yes— oh yes— you may say until Christmas, I suppose.

Well, Mr. Craven, your college seems to be thriving in spite of your want of room &c &c &c &c &c &c &c

Here ends the Extract

The letters and other materials that follow should speak for themselves:

No. Ca. University, Chapel Hill   Feb. 3   1855.[14]
To
The Honorable David S. Reed.
Dear Sir:
I was shown a few moments ago a letter from you to one of our fellow citizens, which is so kind and obliging, that the very style of it induced me to make in my turn an appeal to your well known complaisance.

---

[14] D. S. Reid Papers, vol. III, 1850-1856, p. 360. State Department of Archives and History, Raleigh.

The matter is simply this:

In the month of January 1854, Mr. B. Craven, in the name of the Trustees of Normal College, (over which you then presided *ex-officio*) offered through the newspapers a prize of $200 "for the best essay on the management, regulation and organization of a Literary Institution best adapted to the wants, and interests of North Carolina."

A certain number of essays were sent from different quarters and received by Mr. B. Craven; but no answer of any kind was ever made; the prize has not been awarded, and although it was publicly promised that the name of the judges would be published upwards of six months ago, I am sorry to say that the dissapointed [sic] authors are still awaiting the fulfillment of a pledge which they apprehend to have been made without the knowledge or consent of the gentlemen who then composed the board of Trustees. The fact is that such proceedings are so manifestly unjust and at variance with their well-known principles, and high character, that I take upon myself to apprise you of the whole transaction, hoping that you will have the matter investigated, and justice done to whosoever justice is due.

I remain, Dear Sir,

                Your most obedient and respectful servant
                          Henri Herrisse, A.M.

P.S. Allow me to express the desire of not having my name used in connection with Normal College.

                                  Washington City,
                                  February 6, 1855

My Dear Sir:

I have the honor to acknowledge the receipt of your polite letter of the 3 instant, making inquiry in relation to the prize of $200 offered by Rev. B. Craven, of Normal College, for the best Essay on the organization and management of a Literary Institution in North Carolina.

Altho' the charter of Normal College made the Governor, for the time being, President *ex officio* of the Trustees, yet I never visited the college, nor did I at any time take part in their proceedings. Your letter, I believe, is the first intimation I ever had that such a prize had been offered. I am therefore uninformed about the matter and wholly unable to give you the desired information.

Never having participated in the management of the instution [sic] I do not feel responsible for its action. The nominal connection I had with the college ceased when I went out of the Executive Office. If I had the power to do so I would have the subject to which [you]

allude investigated with a view to having justice awarded to the competitors for the prize.
My best wishes.

> I am, very respectfully,
> Your obt. servant,
> David S. Reid.[15]

Henri Harrisse, Eq.,
Chapel Hill, N. C.

P.S. I presume Mr. Craven would give you information on the subject.

"A PRIZE ESSAY."

The Patriot of the 4th of February, 1854, contained a communication in behalf of "The Trustees of Normal College," proposing to "give $200 for the best Essay on the organization, regulation and management of a Literary Institution best adapted to the wants and interests of North Carolina." The communication was furnished by a friend, and, as we supposed, a Trustee of the College; and was copied from the Patriot into a number of the papers of the State. We heard no more of the matter for some time. But owing, we presume, to our proximity to the Institution, or from the fact that the aforesaid communication first appeared in this journal, there has [sic] recently been various inquiries of us for information on the subject. We can only reply that we know nothing of the matter except what appeared in the communication which we published.

Some two months ago we received a communication from Charleston, S. C., animadverting rather severely on the managers of the College for not complying with their proposition. This Charleston communication was withheld, because we were ignorant of the character of the writer. We have this week received a private letter from a gentleman of this State of the highest respectability, making inquiries on the subject. After stating that information had been sought of him on the subject, the writer of this letter adds:— "Now since the matter has attracted the attention of many persons, both in and out of the State, there should be some public explanation, if any can be given. For as it now stands, there is apparently a breach of faith on the part of the Trustees of Normal College, which might act injuriously to the interests of the College, and, in fact, the character of the Trustees themselves. I wish you would let me know, as early as possible, the truth of the matter. I would be very glad to be able to satisfy the

---

[15] Reid was elected governor of North Carolina in 1850 and served from 1851 to 1854, when he was elected to the United States Senate. It is not clear why as governor he had no part in the activities of Normal College, under whose amended charter of 1852 he was ex officio chairman. Apparently he considered his official relation to Normal College purely nominal.

gentleman above alluded to, who is a citizen of the State and a fine scholar, that all is fair and in good faith."

We would gladly enlighten our friends on this subject, if we could. We hope some friend of Normal College will see the propriety of having the matter explained, which, we presume, can be done to the satisfaction of the public.[16]

PRIZE ESSAY[17]

Normal College, March 6, 1855.

It was determined on consultation, that good and sufficient reasons existed for postponing the adjudication of the Essays, and letters were sent to all persons who had sent essays notifying them to that effect, allowing them the privilege of withdrawing, changing or disposing of their production as they might choose; except in reference to an essay purporting to have come from Baltimore, and a gentleman from South Carolina claiming the control of said essay, called at the College, heard our arrangements, and agreed to the same.

All persons having forwarded essays will be allowed full command of the same; those who are still writing must have them completed in a few months and all in our hands at the appointed time, will be fairly and faithfully judged, and the Premium paid according to the first notice. The shortness of the time allowed to writers, and the difficulty of procuring proper judges have been the chief causes of delay.

We have quite a number of essays on hand, and expect several others. Due notice will be given of the judges and the time of adjudication. Of all the persons interested, we have heard of none dissatisfied except the one mentioned in the Patriot, and I am sure, he would not have been, had he understood the arrangement and acquiescence of so many others equally interested. The very best talent has entered the list, and we hope at no distant day, competent judges will send forth to N. Carolinians, a production worthy the highest consideration. If any now chooses to attach blame to the mode of proceeding, he must not inculpate any Trustee of Normal College except myself; I made the arrangement with the writers, and on the part of the Trustees, am responsible for the result.

B. Craven.

---

[16] *Greensboro Patriot*, March 3, 1855. At the end of the last sentence of the clipping of this article, Harrisse had written, without date: "It never was [explained to the satisfaction of the public]—for the simple reason that it was a regular swindle on the part of that fellow Craven, H."

[17] *Greensboro Patriot*, March 17, 1855.

Raleigh
April 20th, 1855

Sir.

I have the honor to acknowledge the receipt of your favor of the 15th instant together with the statement made by your friend.

I will write to Mr. Craven on the subject and hope that he will see the propriety of promptly returning the essay to the owner or to such friend as he may authorize to receive it.

For the present I do not see that I can do anything more.

With the highest respect

I am sir
Yours truly
Th.s Bragg.

Rev.d F. M. Hubbard,
Chapel Hill

Normal College
April 27, 1855

Mr. Hedrick

Sir

I have the honor to acknowledge your letter directing me to secure a certain Manuscript.

From the description given, I am unable to determine what one may be designated. I think it probable you mean one signed "Excelsior," and it only contains some 75 or 80 pages, those of 100 or more are all marked in some way. I shall be happy to send the Manuscript, if you will designate more closely.

Very respectfully
B. Craven

Raleigh
May 4th, 1855

Sir.

I last evening received a letter from Mr. Craven, President of Normal College, in reply to one addressed by me to him, on the subject of the manuscript essay of your friend— He says that he has written to Prof.r Hedrick that, he will send it to him if he will designate it, as to enable him to select it from many others and that he would have done so before had Mr. H. given him the necessary information. He authorizes me to say that no one has read a line of the essay, and seems indignant that any one should suppose that he would permit a copy to be taken.

Will you allow me to say that I hope the matter may end here— I will not trouble you with my reasons for such a suggestion— I think your own good sense and discretion will furnish enough.

I am sir, Most respectfully and truly yours.

Rev.d F. M. Hubbard,   Th.s Bragg.

HENRY HARRISSE'S NORTH CAROLINA ESSAY

The title page of Henry Harrisse's essay "on the organization, regulation and management of a Literary Institution best adapted to the wants and interests of North Carolina" bears the date of August, 1854. The essay itself is divided into "Part First" and "Part Second" and the author's notes are given in smaller type between rules in the essay. The notes of the editor are used wherever it seems safe for him to presume to identify the persons, books, and things to which Harrisse often alludes in casual and easy manner.

Although the essay itself bears the date of August, 1854, the "Conclusion" to it bears the date of August 10, 1855. The original announcement of the "prize essay" bore the date of January 27, 1854; and the letters and other materials on the controversy that the contest provoked began as early as August, 1854, a year before the date on the "Conclusion." The essay follows:

AN ESSAY "ON THE ORGANIZATION, REGULATION AND MANAGEMENT OF A LITERARY INSTITUTION BEST ADAPTED TO THE WANTS AND INTERESTS OF NORTH CAROLINA."

"Man cannot propose a higher and holier
object for his study than education, and
all that appertains to it."
Plato.

The main object of education consists in disciplining the mind, giving to it habits of activity, spontaneous and continued attention, ready recollection, analysis, generalization; in fine, to teach men to think. It requires no high-wrought arguments to demonstrate this truth, nor elaborate vindications to exonerate it from the attacks of prejudice. It is obvious. And whether we consider the student as "an end unto himself," or his academical career as "an instrument towards some ultimate end," the principle it involves loses none of its authority. This truth, however, is not exclusive; and further, we hold it reconcilable with the well-known dictum of Aristotle, that men, in their youth, "ought to be instructed in things subervient to the purpose of external accommodation, in proportion to their utility or necessity." *

---
* Gillies' Aristotle Polit. B.V.

To others, better qualified to elucidate and harmonize metaphysical abstractions, we leave the task of showing the impossibility of conceiving how the mind can receive impressions, either true or fallacious, abstract or concrete, without retaining indelible traces of the instrument which produced them; and the absolute necessity, therefore, of selecting these instruments, not only as regards their specific worth as training mediums for the time being, but also as channels of knowledge and means to "instruct the student in things subservient to the purpose of external accommodation." Practical questions, when considered too abstractly, – often with the intention of placing them beyond the reach of plain and unassuming thinkers,– or discussed in the abstruse form and wording of philosophical argumentation,– induce distrust, check sincere investigations, and fail to convince. Clothed in logical subtilties, these questions, thus garbled and obscured, may please, perhaps, idle lawyers and presumptuous rhetoricians, but they can never interest the worthy citizen who yields sooner to the dictates of common sense than to the cavils of sophistry.

We will then condense and simplify, as much as we can, whatever recondite notions may occasionally and necessarily spring from the very nature of our subject.

1. Knowledge is necessary to man at all times. How can we realize the idea of reason without assimilating to it the idea of knowledge? You may easily represent to yourself mind without knowledge, as you sometimes think of a steam-engine unsupplied with steam, or the circulatory organs deprived of blood; but from the moment you speak of locomotion, of circulation, of reason, you must add the idea of vapor, of fluid, of knowledge.

We cannot then, deem with Sir William Hamilton,[18] "the mere profession of scientific truths, for its own sake, valueless." *

---

* Sir Wm Hamilton. Discussions on Phil. & Lit. &c Appendix III.

Knowledge is a compound of multifarious materials; and each one of these materials, say, "fact," has a value – not the only value – enhanced or lessened, proportionally as it promotes the intellectual progress of the student. It often happens that of two of these "facts" being equal in point of immediate utility, one possesses inherent qualities denied to the other. As, for instance, a fact, the acquisition of which is an exercise well fitted for sharpening the mental faculties of the student, and at the same time for increasing his individual sum of useful knowledge; whilst the other fact only trains the faculties, and leaves besides nothing but useless knowledge. In this case, is it not self-evident that the former ought not to be preferred to the latter? We should then, in the process of education, so select and employ those facts, as to unfold the mental powers of the student, and simultaneously increase the sum of his useful knowledge.

---

[18] Sir William Hamilton (1788-1856) was a Scottish metaphysician and author of *Lectures on Logic*, and *Discussions in Philosophy, Literature and Education*.

Have our collegiate and academical systems been framed in accordance with the above principles? In no instance can it be said with truth that the training of the mind and the acquisition of necessary information, have been so blended as to promote both. One is, with us, always rendered subservient to the other; and if the course adopted in one institution aims at promoting the training, the other keeps only in view the advancement of the student's scientific attainments. The studies selected in the former result in no ulterior utility whatever, and for the present, (chiefly on account of the mode of teaching) are no better training, perhaps, than other studies, which if properly taught, would certainly both invigorate his mental powers, and increase his acquaintance with facts. In the latter, science, and the application of science to the arts, are the sole objects of their attention; although the instructor does not seem to be aware that his pupils' mind is not yet ready even for the comprehension of such specific facts; which, in consequence, only clog their memory with crude elements; and, if the understanding is not naturally very vigorous, forever impair at least their originality of thought and acuteness of perception.

The range of collegiate studies is far from extensive, nor is it so perfect as not to admit of a change. It would be well then to enquire whether some new studies might not be introduced; others, left out so as to obtain a greater allowance of time, or elevated in point of importance, and taught in a way better calculated to leave a permanent impression upon the pupil's mind. What are the studies that must be abandoned; which ones should be introduced in their stead; what improvements might be successfully applied in the mode of teaching; what is the system of education best calculated to improve the mind of the students, and at the same time leave a residue of knowledge both applicable and useful; in fine, what is the character of the literary institution best adapted to the wants and interests of North Carolina"? Such are the questions which we propose to solve, and, we trust, to the satisfaction of impartial and practical thinkers.

11. All our colleges, universities and classical academies, seem to have adopted a sterotyped course of studies and mode of instruction. From Bowdoin to Austin, and from Wake Forest to St. Vincent's,[19] there is only one curriculum and a uniform method of teaching the same. Is it that these preferred studies possess specific virtues altogether denied to the other branches of human learning, and that with-

---

[19] Bowdoin College in Maine, incorporated in 1794. Austin College was established in Texas in 1849, by the Presbyterians of that state. The establishment of the University of Texas, located at Austin, was not provided for until 1858. Wake Forest College in North Carolina was founded by the Baptist State Convention of that state in the early 1830's. The institution was chartered as an academy in 1834 and as a college in 1838. It may not be clear to what "St. Vincent's" here refers. Vencentians or Lazarists, founded in France in the seventeenth century for missionary and charitable purposes, became identified with Catholic secondary and collegiate education in many countries and established institutions in several places in the United States. Patrick J. McCormick, S.T.L., "Teaching Orders of the Catholic Church," in Paul Monroe, editor, *A Cyclopedia of Education*, V, 529.

out the pale of certain authors and syntax, no science, no literature ever can in an equal degree train the mental powers, impart desirable knowledge, and at the same time promote the graceful and ornamental accomplishments of the student? If it be so in truth, we must lament the narrowness of our resources, and strive by all means to enlarge the circle– but we feel secure on that score.

To impeach the importance of classical studies, is out of the question. When properly and fully taught, and under certain circumstances, they are emphatically the most profitable of all studies. They train several important faculties, and lay open to our eager curiosity the lores of ancient philosophy, poetry and eloquence. Through them we may form our taste, develop our imagination and acquire the only true notions of literary excellence. To obtain such momentous results, however, it is absolutely necessary that they should be studied constantly, fairly and thoroughly, – a partial or interrupted application being altogether worthless, if not hurtful. "A little elementary instruction," says Cousin,[20] "is always good for something, but a little Latin and Greek, badly taught, can be of no advantage, and may even become a source of great inconvenience." *

* Cousin. De l'Instruct. Publ. dans quelques pays de l'Allem. Vol. II.

We justly wonder at the advanced state of German scholarship; but is any one so blind to truth as to imagine that the course followed at Mersburg, at Frankfort or at Grimma, is at all similar to that pursued in Yale or at Princeton?

At Eisenach, Schulpforta, or any of those Gymnasia where the German youth are educated, the students enter the Institution between the age of ten and twelve, having already acquired a certain knowledge both of Greek and Latin, – not so extensive, to be sure, as that required for admission into the Freshman class of our Colleges, but certainly more accurate and better digested. A period of seven years is indispensable to go through the whole course; and, independently of the time devoted to the preparation of the lessons under immediate and constant supervision of responsible monitors or of rigid tutors, they average not less than thirty-two recitations of one hour each a week, whilst in our colleges, they never have more than fifteen.† In

† At the celebrated St. Thomas Schule of Leipzig, the first class has even so many as forty one recitations a week!

---

[20] Victor Cousin (1792-1867), French philosopher and educator, member of the faculty of the University of Paris, member of the Council of Public Instruction in the cabinet of Francois Pierre Guillaume Guizot, and minister of public instruction in France and director of the Normal School. He studied the school system of Prussia in 1831 and published his observations and conclusions under the title *Rapport sur l'état de l'instruction publique en Prusse*, which is among the most important of all reports on educational conditions in Europe in the second quarter of the nineteenth century. It was largely because of this report that the French educational law of 1833 was enacted. The report was translated into English and published in England in 1834, was reprinted in New York the following year, and had considerable influence in this country, especially in Massachusetts and Michigan. Edgar W. Knight, editor, *Reports on European Education*, pp. 114-122.

the first and second years, the German student has only four recitations in Latin and two in Greek, a week; but in the third year the number rises to fourteen in Latin and five in Greek; in the fourth, twelve of Latin, five of Greek; in the fifth, eleven Latin, six Greek; and in the last year nine Latin and six Greek. That is to say, 3000 lessons in the dead languages. In addition, not only the Latin language is spoken, but in the latter part of the course, all the exercises are held in it.*

---

* Cousin, who heard one of these recitations at the gymnasium of Weiman, where they had to translate and explain in Latin, a passage of Plato's Republic, says that the Professors expressed themselves, "justly and forcibly," and the students "fluently and with clearness."

No student can ever pass from a lower class, without sustaining a very strict examination; and it does not follow, as with us, because he has been two sessions a Sophomore, that he must, as a matter of course, enter the Junior Class. Nor do long vacations ever break the link. And yet, all these labors are only preparatory to higher studies. After being graduated at the Gymnasium, the student – if he really designs to master Greek and Latin,– enters the University, and goes through another course in the *Seminarium Philologicum*, which requires several years more, it is true, but which at last enables him to appreciate the beauties of a Homer or the eloquence of a Demosthenes. Then, and only then, the object of his classical education is attained: the treasures of ancient literature are placed within his reach.

Some will answer that the German mind is naturally slow, heavy, turbid, and that it requires such constant efforts to infuse into it, even the first rudiments of any kind of knowledge. Others pretend that they seek only after erudition and obsolete learning. We beg leave to remark, in the first place, that the Germans are neither slow nor turbid; misty they may be, but it is only in their metaphysics, and not in philological researches or the elucidation of classical authors. If they study the dead languages with so much diligence, it is because they are well aware of the necessity of understanding perfectly all the refinements, spirit and genius of a language, whether dead or living, in order to discern the excellence of its poets or prosaists; and as they have found from experience that arduous studies, constant efforts and unremitting attention are absolutely required to become well versed in the classics, they succeeded in framing a system of education which cannot fail to initiate the German student into the sublime excellencies of the Greek and Latin writers.

In the second place, we deem it preposterous to imagine that so enlightened a people as the Prussians certainly are, should strive with so much perseverance to instil nothing but erudition into the mind of all their pupils. Moreover, this far-famed erudition is the result of subsequent and special studies pursued at the Philological Seminaries of Heidelberg, Jena or Berlin.

Admitting even,— were it only for the sake of argument, that the Teutonic youths are dull and altogether unable to acquire any kind of classical learning, unless patiently "hammered into their heads"; to render this objection at all plausible, it will still be necessary to prove, either that so much Latin and Greek is not necessary to appreciate Thucydides and Tacitus, or that with *our* system of education, and the time *we* devote to it, our scholars acquire quite so much learning as the Germans. To refute this, we need only compare the Bowdoin prizes at Harvard or the Berkleian[21] premiums at Yale with the extempore composition in Latin of the *Abiturienten-examen* at any of the 140 gymnasia of Prussia. Why, let any impartial observer who claims to understand anything at all about such literary performances, look over the Latin Salutationes of the First Honor men of our colleges, just as they are handed in to the Professor for revision:— the answer will then be obvious.

Shall we also tax the English and French with slowness of intellect? Yet, they devote several years more than we do to *their Studiæ Humanoriæ*. At Henry IV, St. Barbe or Stanislas, the pupil is likewise subjected to a "Sexennium." Ten hours a day, six days in the week, and eleven months in the year, are wholly occupied with study. We do not recollect at present the exact number of recitations in the dead languages, but it certainly falls not short of that at Pforta or Ratisbon. As for Oxford and Cambridge, every one knows through what ordeals the gownsman has to pass in his Classical Triposes[22] and previous studies under private tutors, before getting his bachelorship. A perusal of the questions asked for the Easter-Term examination of the Freshmen at Trinity, would be of itself sufficient to chill the enthusiasm of our proudest Seniors.

We would not insist, if it had not been promised by very able advocates of the study of the Latin and Greek languages in this country, as superior means of promoting mental habits, that the maturity of these habits is to be measured "by the degree and accuracy of the knowledge."

In point of natural abilities, it is incontestable that the Americans are certainly not inferior to the Europeans. The comfort which our people enjoy; the extensive diffusion of elementary knowledge among all classes; and the freedom of our political institutions, cannot but

---

21 The Bowdoin Prizes at Harvard under the bequest of Governor James Bowdoin, A.B. 1745: "For the advancement of useful and polite literature among the Residents as well graduates as undergraduates of the University. . . ." These prizes "may be conferred for original dissertations in English, Latin, or Greek, or for translations of prescribed passages from English into Latin or Greek." The Berkeley scholarships and prizes at Yale were offered through income from gifts by George Berkeley, who came to Rhode Island in 1729 and who conveyed to Yale College his estate near Newport as a foundation for graduate scholarships and undergraduate prizes.

22 Final honors examinations in the classics.

promote the further acquisition of learning. In proportion to their population, the United States possess, perhaps a greater number of Universities and Colleges, than any one trans-atlantic state, except Prussia; our students commence their education at a more advanced age, and with a maturity of mind far beyond the Germans or French:- How is it, then, that notwithstanding such great advantages and the number of young men we have already educated in the last fifty years, and who have devoted themselves to teaching or Literature, America has not yet produced a single classical scholar, whose philological labors ever drew or merited the approbation of competent and impartial judges,- whilst she can justly boast of astronomers, engineers, and mathematicians equal in many respects to any in Europe? Legare however brilliant and studious, was no Niebuhr, and Dr. Anthon, despite the wide diffusion of his works, or shameless plagiarisms as they may be justly called- is certainly no Boeckh![23] Why are most of our editions of the classics so inferior, and whenever English or German reprints, always clogged with such frothy notes? Why do we find the speeches of our statesmen, the orations, lectures and addresses delivered by our literary characters, uniformly interlarded with trite Latin quotations, - derived no doubt from a Taylor or a Watson, - and hackneyed historical citations, which the most unpretending Sophomore of a Prussian High School would blush to quote? It is in these palpable examples, if no where else, that we must look for the state of scholarship in a country. They alone can tell whether the American system of education really quenches our thirst at the "Pierian spring."

How many of our graduates can read the ancient authors of Rome and Athens in the original, with sufficient ease to enjoy and appreciate them? Alas! but few; and these owe their rare proficiency to subsequent studies and congenial pursuits. If, then, we do not initiate the American scholar into these only repositories of undoubted literary excellence, are we more successful in training their minds through the medium of these very classical studies?

That this can be done, and perhaps more successfully with Thucydides or Juvenal than Euclid or Laplace,[24] is an opinion which Sir

---

[23] Hugh Swinton Legare (1793-1843), American lawyer and statesman, was born in Charleston, was graduated at the College of South Carolina at the age of seventeen, studied law for three years in South Carolina, and then went to Europe where he studied languages in Paris and jurisprudence at the University of Edinburgh. He served for many years in the national House of Representatives and as Attorney-General of the United States, and was appointed Secretary of State *ad interim*. Barthold Georg Niebuhr (1776-1831), German historian and statesman, is said to be among the first students to introduce the scientific spirit and principles into historical study and research. Dr. Charles Anthon (1797-1867) was an American classical scholar and editor of many classical works and handbooks. He served for many years as professor of Greek and Latin at Columbia College, New York City. Philip August Boeckh (1787-1867) was a German classical scholar, professor in the University of Heidelberg and later in the University of Berlin.

[24] Marquis de Pierre Simon Laplace (1749-1827), French astronomer and mathematician, author of the famous *Mécanique Céleste* in five volumes, "a monument in mathematical genius."

William Hamilton and Professor Pillans[25] have very able defended;—but do *we* do it? Can *we* ever do it? Do *we* employ the proper means of doing it?

In what consists our method of teaching the classics? Only in endeavoring to get the student to give the bare meaning of a text. Whether he learns it through the previous reading of an obliging class-mate, his own guessing powers or the memorizing of the passage in one of Mr. Bohn's[26] literal translations, seems to be of no moment to his instructor. In fact, these translations are so openly and universally used, that we venture the assertion that in nine of our colleges out of ten, if a professor in his official capacity, sees any of them in the book-case, upon the table, or in the hands of the student anywhere except in the recitation room, not only does he not reprimand him or seize the book, but considers it not even a breach of discipline worth the trouble of a verbal report to the Faculty. The instructors are so well aware of the fact, that they have contrived a certain plan,—not to check the evil, this seems to be beyond their power,—but to mitigate its effects in a very peculiar manner. They give lessons of four pages instead of two; as if the *quantity* ever could in any way compensate for the *quality;* or as if their main object was to obtain the reading of a certain number of lines without any regard whatever to the *modus operandi.* Now if the study of the dead languages form the bone and sinew of our curricula, because of its specific properties when exclusively applied to the training of the mind, who can deny that in this case the use of translations, whether authorized or illicit, baffles the chief purpose of education, and mocks both teachers and students? If any one doubts, let him peruse the following remarks from one of the highest authorities on Education, Joannes Burton: "When the boy has these helps and incitements to idleness at hand, he will make less use of his own powers of understanding. Assisted by the wealth of others, he will bring nothing from his own store. In a word, he will think it no longer necessary that anything should be done by his own personal exertions; and like an ignorant stranger in an unknown country, submitting to be led by a blundering and treacherous guide, he will wander about without knowing whither he is going." *

---

* **Exord. to Sect. IXth of Vicesimus Knox' Essays.**

It is but just to add, however, that few college instructors willingly tolerate the use of translations; we have even heard it denounced

---

[25] Professor James Pillans was born in Edinburgh in 1778, received his education in the Edinburgh High School, of which he later became rector, and the University of Edinburgh in which he served for many years as professor of humanity and laws. As rector of the Edinburgh High School he introduced the monitorial system of instruction which attracted students and observers from many countries. He wrote on educational subjects and was the author of many textbooks.

[26] Henry George Bohn (1796-1884), British publisher of editions of standard works of history, science, archaeology, theology, the classics and of translations, and dealer in rare books.

from the pulpit; and for an obscure Clarke or Phillips who advocates it, we will find ten celebrated Burtons and Knoxes who loudly reprobate such a pernicious resort to subterfuge and incentive to sloth.

When we say that the study of Latin and Greek exercises and invigorates the mind in a greater degree than some other branches of learning, we attach, we fear, to the word "study," a meaning somewhat different from that generally understood by American instructors. A mere verbal translation, often in impure or disconnected English, with grammatical answers, now and then, is NOT the kind of study calculated to improve greatly the pupil's mental powers. The mind, to derive any profit from a classical course, requires constant appeals to other means of far greater efficacy. Frequent transpositions from Latin into Greek, and from English into Latin; daily written exercises and compositions of verses in these languages; immediate translations into Latin from an English text read aloud; extempore and exegetical readings; turning different dialects into each other, and English verse in Iambic Trimeters &c &c – such are among the multifarious means to which the teacher must resort, if he has truly in view the training of his pupil. It is the method pursued at Leipzig, Paris and Oxford.

Can we, in America, where our children from their very infancy, contract obdurate habits of physical and mental independence, where any kind of restraint is considered a tyranny, and the age of fourteen entirely too early for collegiate instruction, can we ever think of introducing such a system and its necessary train of restrictions and innovations? For, how could we pretend to teach the languages in this way, unless a change of diet, studies in common and under the watchful eyes of rigid tutors, a confinement and catalogue of severe penalties, such as no American youth would ever submit to, were also introduced? Yet, we candidly believe that one is subservient to the other; and in this, lies the secret of the strict discipline so uniformly enforced in all the gymnasia and colleges of Europe.

Admitting even, – again for the sake of argument – that such a severe method can be introduced here, it is useless, and with our old system of instruction we average as many good scholars as they do anywhere in Europe; that if we do not enable the student to read easily, or at all, the Gorgias and the Pharsalia in the original, we marvellously succeed in sharpening his faculties with no other means than verbal translations, – insomuch as four Latin exercises a term at Harvard, one at Yale every two weeks, and a Salutatory Oration once a year in all the other colleges, answer the same purpose;– in fine, that we do not teach the languages either as a specific training, or to lay open the treasures of classical excellence, but only because a knowledge of the Latin and Greek languages, – such knowledge as it may be – is absolutely necessary to understand the etymology of our own, though "it has been ascertained that the English now consists of about 38,000 words, of which 23,000 or nearly five eights are Anglo-Saxon in their origin," * it would still be worth while for us to enquire whether the

* Shaw's Outlines of English Lit. C.I.

establishment of another of these seats of learning where the ancient languages compose the greatest part of the curriculum, would promote in a higher degree the interests, or be "best adapted to the wants of North Carolina."

III. We have neither the time nor the space to discuss at length whether the mind of the student should be especially and wholly trained in view of the particular pursuit he intends to follow in after life; or whether there ought to be only one training for all students, without regard to the profession he may ultimately adopt. It seems to us, however, that although a physician requires a mental discipline altogether different from a lawyer, a merchant from a farmer, and an engineer from a politician, the training preparatory to the acquisition of the specific facts required for the successful prosecution of a profession, should be general. It is necessary to all, and such as no man, whatever be the nature of his ulterior aim, can dispense with.

But, how far, and how long, must the students be subjected to this general training? Is it necessary that the totality of the four years spent in college, should be devoted to it? If so, where and when is he to acquire the knowledge, the bare knowledge, so indispensable to his success in life? We deem it dangerous to leave it to the student to acquire it by himself where and when he pleases; and to postpone it indefinitely is to run too great a risk of his not acquiring it at all. Students should be considered not as they *ought* to be, but as *they are* and ever will be! As soon as they get rid of collegiate shackles,– and often before– they launch at once into the study of a profession. The intended lawyer enters an attorney's office, studies the theory and practice of the Law, hastens to obtain his county court license, and without any further preparation, assumes all the duties and functions of active life. The medical student follows a similar course; and the engineer, whether mentally and bodily prepared or not, immediately enrols himself for a surveying expedition.

On the other hand, has it been fairly tested whether "the instruction in things subservient to the purpose of external accommodation," might not be rendered an excellent mental exercise? And, if so, why not prefer such "utilitarian" studies, since they may simultaneously train the mind and impart the necessary knowledge, which the student "is not expected" to acquire at college, and cannot obtain afterwards,– the functions of active life being too exclusive?

There are sciences, which viewed either in the light of training mediums or of utilitarian studies, are intimately connected with the ulterior actions and thoughts of most men. Who will deny that a thorough study of Whately[27] and Dugald Stewart,[28] under competent instructors and in the proper manner, will enable the student to comprehend better all the intricacies of the Shelley's case,[29] if these, indeed, can ever be understood at all? Can it be doubted that the collegian who engages in the construction of a railroad, already master of Geology, Analytic and Descriptive Geometry, will settle a question in Tennelling, Statics, or Dynamics, more promptly, and perhaps more accurately than even the experienced Engineer who can work it only by the aid of borings, models and **algebraic formulae?**

But, because the methods of fluxions and ratios, are not of paramount use to an agriculturist, or the Reduction of Hypotheticals at all necessary to the welfare of a physician, must we thrust Logic and the Higher Mathematics out of our curriculum; or establish separate colleges for the training of those who expect to pursue different professions? This would be impracticable, if not absurd. Still, let us not be too exclusive, and endeavor so to frame our course of studies as to suit as much as possible the interest of all; which at present is far from being the case. In truth it never was the case. "It seems to be a defect in our system of education," ineffectually said Priestley,[30] more than seventy five years ago, "that a proper course of studies is not provided for gentlemen who are designed to fill the principal stations of *active life,* distinct from those that are adapted to the *learned professions.* We have hardly any medium between an education for the counting house, consisting of writing, arithmetic and merchant's accounts, and a method of instruction in the abstract sciences; so that we have nothing liberal, that is worth the attention of gentlemen whose views neither of these two opposite plans may suit." *

---

* Priestley. Essay on a course of Liberal Educat.

We ask whether these remarks do not apply with as much force to the majority of young men in North Carolina as to the gentry of Lancaster? The necessity of a change in our collegiate system of education is no new topic; and even in the Northern States, where they are so proud of their literary institutions, many a severe pamphlet has been written to censure the course followed in the colleges of New England. We have none of these at hand, but in

---

[27] Richard Whately (1787-1863), English logician and theologian, writer, and professor of political science at Oxford, archbishop of Dublin, author of *Christian Evidences.*
[28] Dougald Stewart (1753-1828) was a Scottish philosopher. He was educated at Edinburgh and served as professor of moral philosophy in that institution.
[29] The reference is to a celebrated and apparently highly complicated but important decision or rule in the law of real property, given or laid down by Lord Chancellor Sir Thomas Bromley in the early 1580's, which operated in the United States as a part of the common law. It was abolished in England in 1925 and by statute has been repealed or modified in several of the American states.
[30] Joseph Priestley (1733-1804) was an English chemist and physicist and writer whose experiments had considerable influence upon the development of chemistry.

referring to President Wayland's[31] Report to the Corporation of Brown University or to Mr. George Ticknor's[32] Remarks on the changes in Harvard College, the reader will see that we do not stand alone in the opinion which we so freely expressed. "Who," asked the celebrated historian of Spanish Literature, "who in this country, by the means offered to him, has been enabled to make himself a good Greek scholar? Who has been taught thoroughly to read, write and speak Latin? Nay, who has been taught anything at our colleges with the thoroughness which will enable him to go safely and directly to distinction, in the department he has thus entered, without returning to lay anew the foundations of his success? It is a shame to be obliged to ask such questions; and yet there is but one answer to them...." *

* Ticknor. Remarks on the Changes in Harvard Col.

Though referring so often to pertinent authorities, and expressing ourselves rather frankly, we do not mean to cast blame upon this or that particular college, either in North Carolina or out of it. Upon the whole, the institutions in the Old North State, are perhaps superior to any in the country. Her University has educated many men who afterwards became eminent; and its alumni do not fall below the standard of American scholarship; but we must confess that neither North Carolina nor any other state in the Union, professes that kind of institution which, having in view both the mental training and the acquisition of useful knowledge, can, through a particular system of instruction, so train its pupils as to enable them to study afterwards any profession whatever with better success; impart the indispensable knowledge which they have not the opportunity of studying when out of college; and, at the same time, give to all those who expect to lead the life of independent farmers, merchants, and citizens, an education that may become from the moment they graduate, an inexhaustible source of literary enjoyment and of materials for thought.

We are well aware that there is hardly a college in the United States which does not lay claim to such a system; but experience has shown, and we hope to have demonstrated, that such is not the case;- however strenuous the effort and meritorious the intention.

---

[31] Francis Wayland, *Report to the Corporation of Brown University, on Changes in the System of Collegiate Education* (Providence, R. I., 1850). In 1842 Wayland had published at Boston *Thoughts on the Present Collegiate System in the United States.* The *Report* recommended some rather radical changes in the collegiate program and both publications stimulated considerable discussion in this country. Wayland, who was president of Brown University for many years, was a strong advocate of the mental disciplinary theory of education.

[32] George Ticknor was professor of Spanish language and literature at Harvard. His *Remarks on Changes Lately Proposed or Adopted in Harvard College,* published at Boston in 1825, was one of the earliest arguments for reform in the collegiate curriculum in this country. Ticknor was greatly impressed with the ideals of German scholarship and thoroughness and intellectual freedom.

Let us take one of our graduates, for instance, either from Yale, Dartmouth or Franklin.[33] If he has been faithful in the prosecution of his collegiate studies, he can read in a day, perhaps, five pages from an easy Greek author,– not however, without irksome and repeated appeals to the lexicon; of Latin, ten pages. In mathematics, he understands many of the propositions in Playfair,[34] Davies[35] or Pierce,[36] but cannot apply the principles involved in them; nor can he solve the examples in Descriptive and Analytic Geometry. Of Logic, he knows but little, and what he understands of Rhetoric is naught, unless being previously endowed with literary taste, he has availed himself of all opportunities to practice writing. His knowledge of Mental Philosophy amounts almost to nothing; – a mere reading of Abbott's Abercrombie or sundry chapters selected here and there in Locke, without any clear and comprehensive lectures to elucidate the principles, give an outline of the History, and show by concise illustrations the "structure," action and characters of metaphysics, – will always prove ineffectual to young students. Now, what has he learnt about History, the most useful, the noblest of all studies? Alas! we dare not answer. On the other hand, has he been taught his own language? Can he write it grammatically, with force and purity? Can he even spell correctly? Ten, twenty, thirty exceptions in a hundred do not alter the case. The welfare of the commonwealth demands that *all* should be at least able to speak and write their mother tongue with perfect accuracy. They all must know the history of their own language; perceive its excellence, feel its force, search its hidden treasures, and be prepared to appreciate the classical monuments of our national literature. We cannot rest satisfied with a show of bombastic and sophomorical periods. We will not call a ridiculous knack of words: elegance, force, eloquence;– a shallow knowledge of Latin and Greek: learning, literary attainments, source of taste and erudition; – a superficial acquaintance with Mathematics and Chemistry: science, practical information, useful knowledge! It is time, high time, that sensible people should cease to repeat with the late Judge Murphey,[37] after a lapse of thirty seven years, that "it is a reproach upon all the literary institutions of our country, that the

---

[33] Franklin and Marshall College had been formed by the union of Franklin College, Lancaster, and Marshall College, Mercersburg, Pennsylvania. There were also Franklin College, Franklin, Indiana, 1844, and Franklin College in New Athens, Ohio; and Franklin College was the early name of the University of Georgia.
[34] Charles Playfair (1748-1819) was a Scottish mathematician and physicist.
[35] Charles Davies (1798-1861), author of a well-known and widely used series of textbooks on mathematics.
[36] Benjamin Osgood Peirce (1809-1880) was an American astronomer and mathematician.
[37] Archibald D. Murphey (1777-1832), eminent North Carolina jurist, pioneer in educational and economic reforms, "father of the common schools" of that state, whose report on education (1817) offered the first definite proposal for a public school system in North Carolina.

course of studies pursued in them teach most young men only how to become literary triflers." *

* Judge Murphey. Reports to the Legislat. of No. Ca. (Nile's Regist. 1819)

To conclude:
The increasing prosperity of North Carolina; the late discovery of rich mines; the building of important railroads; the impulse given to internal improvements; the constant endeavors of the Legislature to promote education; and, above all, the spirit which after a slumber of many years, now pervades her people, will effectuate ere long, such a transformation as never was before witnessed in any State. Be prepared for that great renovation; educate your young men in view of the coming progress; enable them to second the impulse, and you shall not prove inefficient to exalt North Carolina to that lofty station among her sister States, which she always deserved, and, we hope, will not fail soon to occupy!!

PART SECOND

"For if you will have a tree bear more fruit than it hath used to do, it is not anything you can do to the boughs, but it is the stirring of the earth, and putting new mould about the roots, that must work it." (Bacon)

"SHOULD THE INSTITUTION BE A COLLEGE, ACADEMY, HIGH SCHOOL &c &c?"

I. Our Institution resembles neither a College, an Academy, nor a High School; but as we should avoid introducing foreign words or coining new terms, we adopt the word "College" as the nearest we can find in the English language. Johnson and Bailey[38] define it "a number of persons acting or living under the same laws and the same rules; applied especially to those who devote themselves to learning or religion." Learning "consists in the knowledge of facts imparted through instruction and study," says Webster. It is self-evident that the object of our Institution is to collect a number of persons willing to live under the same rules, in order to devote themselves to learning;– which we purpose to impart to them through instruction. We may then, in all propriety, employ the word "College," though we should reject certain branches of learning usually taught in collegiate institutions.

Being convinced that the study of the Latin and Greek languages – (as now taught and as they will ever be taught in this country–) does

[38] Nathan or Nathaniel Bailey (d. 1742), English philologist and lexicographer, who published in 1721 *An Universal Etymological English Dictionary* which Samuel Johnson (1709-1784), English writer and lexicographer, is said to have used liberally in preparing his famous *Dictionary of the English Language* which appeared in 1755.

not enable the student to read the classical authors with sufficient ease in the original to appreciate their literary excellence, and use them as models of taste and style, or vehicles of information; and that considered specially as a means of mutual training, this study when partially taught does not discipline the mind in a higher degree than other studies which, besides professing this quality, may also impart a great deal of useful and necessary knowledge, the Greek and Latin languages form no part of our curriculum.

That which we substitute instead, is neither new nor obsolete. It consists merely in extending several of the very studies pursued in all the literary institutions of this country, adding a few others, and adopting a method of instruction which exacts more from both student and instructor. Through this method, the whole sum of physical and mental application which can be expected from an American youth in educational pursuits, will be obtained.

The vast amount of time hitherto devoted to an imperfect acquisition of the dead languages, we transfer to a profound study of our own language and literature, a foreign tongue universally spoken, that can be acquired in a few years, and which at the same time trains the mental powers in a satisfactory degree; a comprehensive study of History, both ancient and modern; Drawing and Penmanship, Mental Philosophy, Logic, Constitutional Law, Political Economy, Mathematics, Natural Philosophy, Chemistry, Geology and Gymnastics, complete the course.

"THE NUMBER, QUALIFICATIONS AND DUTIES OF THE TEACHERS."

II. The Faculty to whom are committed the government and instruction of the students, consists of seven members, viz: a Professor of Mental Philosophy, Political Economy and Constitutional Law. This chair is filled by the President:— a Professor of French Language and Drawing; a Professor of History, Antiquities and Geography; a Professor of Mathematics and Natural Philosophy; a Professor of Chemistry, Geology and Minerology; an adjunct Professor of English Literature; and an Instructor in Gymnastics who also fills the office of Marshall. The youngest member of the Faculty is ex-officio, Secretary of the body.

As soon as the endowment will allow it, assistant professors will be added to all the departments, except the English.

The qualifications of the teacher are naturally to be sought in his proficiency to teach the branch of science or learning entrusted to him. And to repeat here, that he must be a thorough master of his Department; accustomed both to teach and study, — "for the one exclusive sign of a thorough knowledge is the power of teaching" — a strong friend of the institution; a man who is ever above the petty selfishness and jealousy which so often prevail among the members of academical senates and looks upon the profession of teacher, more as the discharge of a noble, *life time* and solemn duty, than a make-shift or means of temporary support, would perhaps appear trite or idle. There are, no doubt, some specific requisites which we must expect from our Instructors; these, however, will be defined under the head of "Method of Instruction."

The moral qualities of a teacher have always been a subject of earnest enquiry; and as it would be the height of presumption in us to comment upon a topic so completely investigated by such men as Quinctillian [sic][39] Burton, Locke and Rollin, we beg leave to answer the above query, by a quotation from the great Roman rhetorician.

"Let the master above all things," says Quinctillian, "bear towards his scholars the affection of a parent, and look upon himself as succeeding to the place of those who have delivered them over to his care. Let his discipline be without asperity, and his indulgence without cheapness; thus he will secure their affection, and avoid their contempt. Though far from being passionate, yet he is not to dissemble whatever requires amendment. Let him be plain in teaching, patient of labor, and punctual rather than precise. Let him readily answer the inquisitive, and of himself examine those who are otherwise. In commending the exercise of his pupils he ought neither to be niggardly nor lavish, because the first begets disgust, the other negligence." *

---

* **Guthrie's Quinctillian B. 11. ch. 2.**

As for the duties of the teachers, there is hardly a digest of collegiate by-laws, which does not clearly define them. These rules constitute the whole amount of experience ever gathered on the subject of education; and they have so often been revised, corrected and improved, that we deem the digest of any college whatever as good a compendium as can be desired. In fact, the instructor's duties, from the humble assistant of an "old field" teacher to the dignified professor in a State University, are similar in the main; and differ only in those unimportant particulars, which arise from the peculiar locality, or importance, of the Institution.

They all declare that it is his duty to inspect the conduct of the students within the college walls; to see that the hours of study and retirement are faithfully observed, the students not out of their rooms at improper times; that the quiet of the campus is not disturbed by noises, shouts, or boisterous calls; to suppress all disorderly conduct; examine in turn the rooms of the college at least once a week, and see that cleanliness and neatness are preserved. In fine, he must be vigilant in carrying into effect any law of the institution and report to the Faculty, such transgressions as ought to be punished by that body.

---

[39] Marcus Fabius Quintilianus (35-93 A.D.) was a distinguished Roman rhetorician whose *Institutio Oratoria* is considered one of the greatest treatises on a liberal education. Harrisse puts a "c" and an extra "l" in the name.

He is not permitted to engage in pursuits for emolument unconnected with the service of the College; and, if a clergyman, cannot take charge permanently of any church, in or out of the village where the Institution is located.

"THE POWERS AND DUTIES OF THE TRUSTEES"

III. A Trustee is generally a retired public officer, a gentleman of leisure or an influential lawyer who knows but little and cares still less about the management of a literary institution. His title was conferred as a mere compliment, or on account of his well known abilities in other pursuits. Often, however, it is simply by reason of his high-sounding name. We know of such trustees who have been figuring in college catalogues for twenty years, without ever attending a single monthly or annual meeting.

Our trustees are men of experience and activity. We do not wish a numerous board, but a few diligent members who are required and never fail to attend, all the regular examinations; thus adding by their presence, importance to a ceremony which in some colleges is rapidly degenerating into a solemn mockery.

The number of trustees is limited to ten. The President of the college is ex-officio a member, has a vote, but is ineligible to the office of chairman of the Board. He, however, with four of the trustees, can call occasional meetings whenever it appears necessary. Six members and the President of the college are the number to constitute a quorum, and to fill up, by ballot, any vacancies that may occur either in the Board or in the Faculty.

The trustees elect, and may remove from office, the President and all the officers connected with the Institution.

They prescribe and amend the course of studies to be pursued by the students. They meet regularly at the end of each term, and individually visit the college by turns at least four times in the year.

They have the exclusive right of expelling a student; and may reverse all sentences of suspension pronounced by the Faculty. All other penalties, their degree and mode of infliction, are wholly left to the Faculty. We need not add that corporeal punishments of any sort are strictly prohibited.

The Trustees confer degrees; and if anyone fails to attend the board during four stated meetings in succession, it is deemed a refusal to act, and the board proceeds to appoint a successor; except of course in case of sickness or temporary absence from the State at the time.

"RULES AND REGULATIONS FOR TEACHERS AND STUDENTS"

IV. Here again, as in chapter II, we must refer to the digest of any collegiate by-laws; leaving to the teachers themselves, whatever local alterations may prove necessary. As for sundry regulations which we wish to introduce, they will be found at length in the chapter treating of the method of instruction, and others. These new regulations are not so numerous as to require a separate chapter; and if we ventured to sum them up under one head before exhibiting an outline of the system, they would appear totally disconnected, and perhaps, unintelligible or trifling.

One, however, we beg leave to expatiate upon. It is the extreme facility with which a student is so often permitted to pass from one class to another, without professing even the amount of knowledge strictly necessary to understand the studies of his own class. In American colleges, we frequently see students who scarcely ever study during the session. They get one of their classmates to read over the lesson to them whenever there is a probability of being "called up." If they fear that on account of their constantly bad recitations they run the risk of being brought before the Faculty,– which rarely proves of any avail–; marked "bad" on the report, or "disapproved"– which is seldom the case, though often apprehending it– they devote themselves during a day or more, perhaps, to an earnest and unwholesome study of their text books. Thus cramming and "reviewing" that which they never before learned; and by dint of close application during a short time, abundance of literal translations and the friendly assistance of learned class-mates, they save themselves from a mere though apparently serious, threat of rustication or dismissal.

We use the words "mere threat" because it has become of late a prevailing opinion in some institutions, that a great number of students is the only evidence of the prosperity of a college, – thus forgetting "that the intrinsic excellence of a school is not to be confounded with its external prosperity, estimated by the multitude of those who flock to it for education." * To be better able to issue yearly

---

* Hamilton. Discussions. App. 111.

---

a crowded catalogue, they leniently admit candidates who are deficient in some studies under the pretence that they may afterwards "make up" – as if the college course and every day's task were not already sufficiently difficult and absorbing, to engross all their time; – add the names of those who have left the Institution, or been expelled, or deceased for some time; and often slide over offences which would be punished severely, if thereby their singular scale of collegiate prosperity were not to show a decrease by the omission of a few names.

Whether it is possible for any student to require in two days what is deemed necessary by sensible persons to study during five months is one of those questions which may be solved in a satisfactory manner when we consider how many ignorant students do graduate, and how few are turned out of college as deficient in scholarship, though deserving it. Now, there is not perhaps a single evil in the whole catalogue of collegiate nuisances which, so loudly calls for immediate censure and extirpation.

The attention of European professors has long been awakened on the subject for it is a mischief which at one time reigned there likewise; but by energetic measures they have succeeded at last in palliating its pernicious consequences. In many colleges it is totally eradicated.

"In Prussia," says Mr. Cousin," a salutory severity presides over the admission of the student into another division. With us, the Imperial Regulations also prescribe two examinations in the year, but these, as well as many others, are not enforced (1831); so much so that the higher classes are sometimes filled with students who are not able to follow the course therein pursued. Outwardly it does very well; the classes are numerous, the receipts large and the college has the appearance of being in a prosperous condition; but at bottom, there are only a dozen students who profit by the instruction. On the contrary, enforce the regulations, and by strict examinations close the entrance of the higher classes to the students who are not able to profit by them, it will subject to constant studies those who wish to be admitted, and cast out of college after a few trials, those who will have been thus convicted of not being fitted for literary and scientific studies. There will be a smaller number of students in the higher classes, but these will be able to follow the Professor's lessons; their knowledge will faithfully represent the degree of proficiency which they have attained; and both the parents and the community, will know what to think of it." *

---

* Cousin. Instr. Publique. Conclusions.

These remarks from such high authority, cover the whole ground. We have nothing to add.

"THE AMOUNT AND METHOD OF INSTRUCTION."

V. There is only one session, which commences on the first Friday in September, and continues forty-five weeks, including public speaking, examinations and Commencement.

The session is divided into three terms of fifteen weeks, at the end of which terms all the classes are examined by divisions in presence of the Trustees and Faculty. In this way, a frequent opportunity is offered to the students who have been successful in the prosecution of their studies, to pass into a higher section; and an annual vacation of seven weeks is secured. This is more than sufficient. In the Royal Colleges of France, where a greater amount of study and confinement is required of the collegians, they have only one month,— but we must make allowances for the nature of our pupils, their habits, and the bad condition of our Southern roads.

Let no smile of incredulity play on the lips of our readers; an imperious necessity demands that collegiate vacations should be shortened in duration, and less frequent. In themselves, these vacations are productive of good,— the bow keeps on the stretch better from being occasionally unstrung,—but when recurring often, the perturbation they occasion in the studies is too great. The very anticipation of them makes itself felt; and it takes at least two weeks to settle the mind of the student after his return. We have introduced then, only two holidays, viz—. Christmas, which lasts ten days, appointed by the Faculty, and the 1st day of April.

The public speaking of the graduating class takes place the very week preceding Commencement. No member of the other classes, declaim publicly on the occasion. The number of students is limited to two hundred. It can never be increased; even with the addition of professors and buildings. The students are divided into four classes called Freshmen, Sophomores, Juniors and Seniors. Each one of these classes is subdivided into two divisions. The first division consists of the more advanced scholars; and at the end of each term, those of the second division who have stood a satisfactory examination join the first division; those who have not, remain where they are; or after one more unsuccessful trial in the same division are dismissed. This system we are told works well at West Point; and we do not see why it should not meet with a like success in our college. By these means, the more attentive students proceed rapidly and are not thwarted in their career by the "gentlemen of leisure" whom President Barnwell[40] is reported to have said, we must expect to admit and retain, and endure, and graduate, in all the institutions throughout the length and breadth of this blessed country.

The classes recite and hear the lectures by divisions. They study by sections of one fourth of the whole class, when it numbers 50; of one third when less than forty.

All the students, *Seniors not excepted*, have three recitations a day during five days in the week; on Saturday they recite twice, and Sunday only once. Monday and Saturday mornings are set apart for Drawing; the former on account of the Sabbath evening, and the latter of the Debating Societies, which prevent the preparation of a recitation for the following morning.

As in all other colleges, they have prayer every day at Sun rise and at Sun down; and service in the Chapel on Sundays.

---

[40] Robert W. Barnwell (1801-1882) became president of the College of South Carolina in 1835, succeeding Thomas Cooper, whose theological liberalism or radicalism had greatly reduced or had threatened to reduce the prestige of that institution.

The hour from 12 to 1 P.M. every day, is devoted to Gymnastic exercises, which are obligatory upon all students.

The whole number of recitations amount to 2756–, which are thus divided among all the departments;

	English Gram. Literat. Rhetoric Logic	Mathematics Nat. Philosophy	Antiquities, History	Geography	French Langua. and Literature	Intel. Philosophy Polit. Economy, Const. Law.	Chemistry Geology &c.	Drawing	Bible Mor. Science
Freshmen.	4.	4.	3	1	3.	"	"	2	1. a Week
Sophomores.	4	4.	3.	"	2	"	2	2.	1. "
Juniors.	4	4.	3	"	2	"	2	2	1. "
Seniors.	3	"	1	"	2	7	2	2	1. "
	559.	463.	386.	38.	347	270	231	308	154.

DEPARTMENT OF ENGLISH GRAMMAR LITERATURE AND
COMPOSITION; ELOCUTION RHETORIC & LOGIC.

It is a remarkable fact that many of the American statesmen and politicians who have had the advantage of a collegiate education, write their mother tongue with less perfection than might be expected. Their style is often forcible, their logic overpowering, and none of their stirring appeals ever fail in effect; but if we lay aside our admiration or partiality, patriotism or party-spirit to analyse the rhetorical part of their orations, we find that the words in themselves are not of the purest choice, whilst the sentences are rarely framed with taste and simplicity. Their diction is energetic, but irregular, and frequently lacks grammatical accuracy. How few of the celebrated speeches which have stirred the souls of all hearers either within the Halls of Congress or on the Public Squares, but appear to us who are not under the spell of the orator's eloquent accents, cold stiff and disconnected. Is it so with Bossuet's[41] Panegyrics or Burke's speeches?

Many, if not all, of our periodicals are written in very indifferent English. In fact, we know only of Mr Joseph Gale's[42] editorials, which can be compared for purity of style to a London Times' leader; and though allowances must be made for the provincialisms, newly coined words, cant terms, which always will creep into political arguments or newspaper controversies it must be conceded that a better choice of words and more carefully wrought sentences, might be used in all our public prints: inasmuch as the majority of editors are Alumni of our colleges.

We ascribe this defect to the little attention paid to the study of English Grammar and Rhetoric. When do we recite in Murray[43] or Fowler? Only at the Preparatory school simultaneously with Bullion and Andrews. Why, in many instances, we never open an English grammar after we have passed the age of twelve; we even look upon it then with indisguised contempt. The little we learn in after life about the structure and character of our native language is wholly derived from a kind of involuntary imitation. "If any one among us have a facility or purity more than ordinary in his mother tongue" said Locke,* "it is owing to chance or his genius or anything, rather

---

* Locke. Of Education. 189.

---

than to his education or any care of his teachers." It is true in all our colleges the Professor of Rhetoric faithfully corrects whatever errors, both of style and grammar, he may detect in the compositions of his

---

[41] Jacques Benigne Bossuet (1627-1704), French divine, writer, bishop of Meaux, and celebrated pulpit orator.
[42] Joseph Gales (1761-1841) was born in England, came to this country in the latter part of the eighteenth century, and in 1799 founded in Raleigh, North Carolina, the *Raleigh Register*, a weekly Jeffersonian journal, which he edited with high distinction until 1832.
[43] Lindley Murray (1745-1826), American grammarian.

pupils, but we should not lose sight of the fact, that the student enters college with an exceedingly scanty knowledge of his own language; and the arrangements are such, that he can write compositions only once in three weeks; and even then he aims more at sophomoric periods than grammatical accuracy. What our pupils imperiously want, consists in a firm and broad basis; in principles never to be forgotten, and imparted through a simple method, which speaks louder to the understanding than to the memory.

A rule of grammar is almost as complex as a metaphysical abstraction; read the Hermes,[44] peruse the Divisions of Purley! In truth, it is nothing but an abstraction; and there is such a great difference between inculcating principles of this sort through a mere mechanical process, to lie dormant in the memory until age and necessity unfold them to your astonished understanding, or by mental exertions, proportioned to your wants and abilities, that we gladly avail ourselves of this opportunity to elevate the study of the English *grammar* to a station worthy of its importance;— The sneers of pedants, and the contemptuous smiles of college snobs to the contrary notwithstanding.

We constantly praise a Chaucer and a Milton, a Bollingbroke and a Burke; but are we thoroughly, or at all, acquainted with their writings? Are we even prepared to appreciate the style and genius of these master spirits of our vernacular literature? Alas! we often do not read their works at all; and when we do so, it is only in after life, without any guide to point out the beauties, or make us feel the sublimity of their masterly compositions. It is not sufficient to peruse books, were it with the most unrelenting attention, to be at once qualified to perceive their excellence. A certain discriminating taste and respectable acquaintance with the principles of Rhetoric, are necessary to judge of the merits of any literary production whatever. This power of sound criticism is not altogether innate, – at least in the state required for its immediate application. It is unfolded, if not required, only by constant and enlightened comparisons with well selected models; judicious analysis and critical observation under the guidance of an experimental teacher.

The college is the place to obtain these first principles; and we are so convinced of their importance, that neither time or attention is spared in our Institution, to ground them deeply in the student's mind.

In this department, we devote three lessons a week during the three terms of the Freshman class to a comprehensive study of the Grammar, and one every five days to the writing of an original composition, setting forth in a prescribed manner the syntactic principles studied during the week, and the preceeding, – but no other.

In the Sophomore year, a work on Rhetoric (Whaley's), and another

---

[44] Pertaining to Georg Hermes (1775-1831), German Roman Catholic theologian, professor of theology in the University of Bonn.

on criticism (Kame's)[45] together with appropriate lectures, exhibiting the history, character and philosophy of language, together with a composition absorb the four recitations allotted every week during the whole year to this department.

In the Junior class, they also write a composition, and read select passages from English classical authors, which they analyse orally in presence of the whole division. Any student can read thirty pages of Atterbury or one act of Ben Johnson in two hours. Now 4000 pages well chosen from among our standard writers, and elucidated in the above manner, cannot fail, it strikes us, to initiate the student into the merits of the English Literature.

Logic is with us a last study, absorbing two recitations a week during the first and second terms of the Senior class. It is time that our pupils should be convinced of the importance of Logic, and be shown that it is a highly useful study, which, when properly taught, trains the mind of the older members of college better than any other.

The third recitation in the three terms is devoted to the Professor's criticisms upon the speeches written during the week; and the two last recitations of the third term, to the history of English Literature. Twenty-five lessons are more than sufficient for a careful study of Shaw's Outlines.

DEPARTMENT OF MATHEMATICS, NATURAL PHILOSOPHY
AND ASTRONOMY.

Without sharing entirely the utter scepticism of Sir William Hamilton, or the excessive enthusiasm of Dr. Whewell as regards the excellence of mathematical studies, we believe with the former that mathematics have been greatly overrated as an invigorating exercise of the reasoning faculties; and readily grant to the latter, that this science considered in itself, or "in its subjective results," as Sir William is wont to say, must be left, at least as a co-ordinate, to find its level among the other branches of academical instruction.

The principal ground upon which we introduce Mathematics into our scheme is not then, as many Cantabrigians candidly affirm, because they are means of forming logical habits better than logic itself; or similar reasons based altogether upon partiality or fancy. This would be preposterous in the extreme, especially at this time, when nearly every body has perused the remarkable dissertation of Hamilton on the subject, and lent credence to the crowd of unimpeached and unimpeachable authorities, from Descartes to Newton, which he adduces to support his arguments. We appeal to better reasons, and shelter ourselves under the "ancient and universal observation" that as different studies cultivate the mind to a different development, the

---

[45] The reference may be to Lord Henry Home Kames (1696-1782), Scottish lawyer and philosopher who wrote on many subjects and was the author of *An Introduction to the Art of Thinking* and *Elements of Criticism*.

end of a liberal education should be "the general and harmonious evolution of its faculties and capacities in their relative subordination"; – and it is incontestable that the study of Mathematics, without being at all a specific, is a useful exercise of intelligence, which may unfold several of these very faculties.

The student is admitted into the Freshman class with a competent knowledge of Arithmetic and the simple Equations of Algebra. We carry him through the equations of the First degree, and the whole of Euclid in the first year.

Logarithms, Plane Trigonometry, Navigation, Analytical (Bourdon's in the original) and Descriptive Geometry are studied in the Sophomore year. Too little attention is paid to the latter in our colleges; yet it is a study which may sharpen the mental powers quite as well as Analytics, and is by far the most useful to any but future Astronomers. It is for the want of Descriptive study and drawing that such general ignorance prevails among pretty well educated men with regard to plans and sections of Buildings, Machinery, Works of arts &c &c. They seem utterly incomprehensible to them. They cannot realise how one plane can cut another and be represented all on one plane.

Differential and Integral calculus (Boucharlat's in the original) Natural Philosophy (Young's) and Astronomy complete the mathematical course; which we believe from experience, can be gone through with the 463 recitations allotted to this department; – including the necessary lectures and experiments on Hydrostatics, Pneumatics, Magnetism &c.

In the Junior year, not less than twenty hours, taken from ten different nights are devoted to a practical application of Astronomy.

And, so as to improve the powers of continued attention, we adopt the suggestion of Dugald Stewart viz:– to accustom the student to pursue long trains of demonstrations without availing himself of the aid of any sensible diagrams, "the thoughts being directed solely to those ideal delineations which the powers of conception and of memory enable us to form." *†

---

* Dougald Stewart. Elm. of Phil. 1. pt- ch. IV.

† Pestalozzi used the above method with perfect success, and the superiority of the graduates of the Polytechnic school is partially ascribed to this system of studying Mathematics.

[Johann Heinrich Pestalozzi (1746-1827), famous Swiss educational reformer, whose influence was very extensive in the United States, especially after 1860. Harrisse, in his statement above that "the end of a liberal education should be 'the general and harmonious . . .,' is obviously attempting to recollect Pestalozzi's well-known definition of education as "the natural, progressive and harmonious development of all the powers and faculties of the human being."]

Department of Antiquities, History and Geography

3. When Priestly [sic] was only a poor and unknown tutor in a poor and unknown academy at Warrington, he wrote an Essay "on a course of liberal education for civil and active life" which might still be read with advantage. In this remarkable performance, he earnestly inveighs against the course of education then pursued in England; and points out faults which neither his just remarks nor the experience of nearly a century, have succeeded in alleviating in the least.

After showing that the difficulty is how to fill up with benefit those years which immediately precede a young man's engaging in the higher spheres of active life in which he is distined to move, what does he recommend as the new article of academical instruction "having a nearer and more evident connection with the business of active life, and which may therefore bid fair to engage the attention and rouse the thinking powers of young gentlemen of active genius"?*
History, Civil History!

---

* Priestley. Essay on Educat. p. 1.

And so it should be. History tends to invigorate the sentiment of virtue, and enables us to form just ideas both of the strength and weakness of human nature; it is a pleasing and interesting study which serves to amuse the imagination, and interest the passions; it improves the understanding; evinces facts essential to all knowledge; frees the mind from many prejudices; and in fine fits men for the business of life. These reasons are Priestley's, and spring from common-sense.

Now, peruse the catalogue of any American college, and see how limited is the place this important study holds in the Curriculum! We are aware of only two regular and special professorships of History in the United States; one of which, the McLean, at Harvard, is not and perhaps never was, filled. In the other colleges it is added as a fifth wheel in a wagon; and at the University of Virginia, where they ought to know better, History is hardly taught at all.

With us, the Freshmen recite in Weber's Outlines, and Bogesen's Antiquities.

The Sophomores in Antiquities and Tytler's Universal History.

The Juniors in Hume's History of England and American Constitutional History. During the Senior year, they write original Hist. Dissertations.

Geography is mostly taught in the Freshman class, and occupies 38 recitations. These, together with the amount of geographical knowledge required for admission, and the constant references made in connection with the historical course during the three following years, are amply sufficient to render the student, if not a thorough master at least a respectable adept, in this useful branch of knowledge.

Without thinking with Vossius[46] and Locke, that maps ought to be intrusted to boys so early as the age of six, we are so convinced that engravings, globes &c., greatly exercise the eyes and memory, and accelerate the improvement of the scholar in presenting new ideas clearly to his apprehension, that not only all our halls and recitation rooms are furnished with these implements, but during the Sophomore year, half of the drawing lessons are devoted to geographical sketches and maps. In the Junior class the student is often required to draw on the blackboard, whilst the recitation is going on, plans of cities, the march of armies through conquered countries &c. &c. so as to blend as much as possible, Geography with History.

DEPARTMENT OF THE FRENCH LANGUAGE AND LITERATURE

4. It is often urged that the chief excellence of the dead languages consists in training the mind to a higher degree than any other study. Why? Is it on account of the peculiar nature of the Greek and Latin idioms and syntax, or because the study of any language whatever calls forth the strongest and most unexclusive energy of thought? The first of these reasons is certainly plausible, though the grammatical structure of these two languages, always appeared to us much simpler than the French participles or German paradigms, but we are not aware of its having ever been urged, except in the easy form of mere association. Stephanus and the philologists of old, who so earnestly advocated and did so much for the study of the Greek and Latin, aimed not at proving their educational virtues, which is a consideration altogether of modern origin. It was the richness, the force, the euphony, the literature which they justly and loudly praised. As for the second reason, it is founded on truth. The grammatical intricacies of all languages are nearly akin, and to overcome them requires the same faculties. Every argument which can be adduced on that score in favor of the Greek and Latin languages, will apply with equal force to any modern language whatever. With this difference, that a spoken tongue is always better understood and taught than a dead one. As we need that peculiar kind of training which the study of a language alone can give, it remains to make a choice.

If we look only for barren difficulties, the Chinese, with an endless variety in its collocation of unchangeable roots, must be preferred to the German, and the German to the French. But common-sense tells us that the difficulties we seek are not of the sort; and the first claim which a language should have on our choice, lies in its utility, perfection and literature.

The German or the Spanish, then, might be taught with advantage.

---

[46] Gerhard Johann Vossius (1577-1649), German classical scholar and theologian.

The former, on account of its copiousness and the affinities it bears to our own language; the latter, because of its importance to Southern students, and the richness of its idiom, which could not fail ultimately, if generally read and spoken, to work a desirable change in the euphony of the English tongue. But, as we do not wish our students to possess only a smattering, but a thorough acquaintance with ONE foreign language, we do not follow the example of the New York University, and others, where they are taught, *nolens volens*, French in the Freshman class, German in the Sophomore, and Italian and Spanish. Let any one that has ever attempted to study a modern language at College, state how much he has learnt in one, in two, in three years! No, only one of these languages is taught in our Institution, but we expect our students to be able by the time they are graduated, to read, to write, and perhaps speak it with ease and accuracy.

As the choice of this one language is vested in us, we select the French.

Locke remarks that the pupil should learn some other language than his own; "this nobody doubts of," says he, "when French is proposed." * The reasons are obvious, if we believe Vicesimus Knox:[47]

---

* Locke. 162.

"The French Language abounds with authors elegant, lively, learned and classical. A scholar cannot in this age, dispense with it. To be ignorant of it, is to cut off a copious source of amusement and information. I need not expatiate on its utility to the man of business, and the ornament it adds to the accomplished gentleman. Its use and its grace are sufficiently understood." †

---

† Vicesimus Knox. Liberal Educat. Sect. XV.

In this Department, the recitations of the Freshman Class are devoted to the Grammar and written exercises.

In the Sophomore year they read Voltaire's Charles XII and St. Pierre's *Etudes de la Nature*.[48]

In the Junior year, Racine and Corneilles's Tragedies and Moliere's Comedies. The grammar used in this class is Chassal's in the original.

In the Senior, they read extracts from Marot, Montaigne and the early writers. The 3rd term is exclusively devoted to the History of French Literature.

Throughout the course, they study the grammar, write exercises and memorize colloquial sentences. Lectures are occasionally delivered

---

[47] Vicesimus Knox (1752-1821), English divine, popular and voluminous writer on miscellaneous subjects.
[48] Bernardin de Saint-Pierre (1737-1814), Frenchman of letters and engineer, who was influenced by Rousseau. His *Etudes de la Nature*, which appeared in three volumes in 1784, "was an attempt to prove the existence of God from the wonders of nature."

in the vernacular tongue; and once a month, on Saturday, the Junior and Senior classes, hold conferences by sections, in which the French language is exclusively spoken.

DEPARTMENT OF CONSTITUTIONAL LAW, POLITICAL ECONOMY AND MENTAL PHILOSOPHY.

5. However strange it may appear to the most lenient observer, in all our Colleges it is at the very time when the student's mind is ready to unfold itself fully, and to derive benefit from three years training, that they relax the discipline and lessen the studies to which, he was hitherto subjected. From the moment he gets to be a Senior, he may linger in bed whilst his college-mates are at work; and has only ten recitations a week instead of fourteen.

With us, the Senior studies are the most arduous, the lessons the longest; and besides the lectures, the members of this class recite thrice a day.

During the first term and part of the second, three recitations a week are devoted to the Statute law of North Carolina and Story's[49] Commentaries on the Federal Constitution.

It has been hinted that self-government is a kind of intuitive knowledge with us. This we do not doubt.– Are not the Americans the chosen people? But we nevertheless deem it necessary to our young men to study carefully under the supervision of a very able and impartial instructor, both our State Laws and the United States Constitution.

"In a country where free institutions prevail and where public opinion is of consequence," says Sir John Herschel in his well-known letter to Dr. Adamson, "every man is to a certain extent a legislator; and for this his education (especially when the government of the country lends its aid and sanction to it) ought at least so far to prepare him, as to place him on his guard against those obvious and popular fallacies which lie across the threshold of this as well as of every other subject with which human reason has anything to do. Every man is called upon to obey the laws, and therefore, it cannot be deemed superfluous that some portion of every man's education should consist in informing him what they are!" * Judge Story's

---

* Discussions. 712.

---

interpretations are often tainted with party spirit, but where can we find in works accessible to students, a clearer exposition of our complex system of constitutional checks and balances?

In the second term, they study Political Economy, – a capital antidote for some of Story's doctrines.– Wayland, together with Bastiat's

---

[49] Joseph Story (1779-1845), jurist, and associate justice of the Supreme Court of the United States.

Sophismes (in the original) are our text books. The main reason for our selecting Wayland in preference to Say, is that he sums up the elements of the science in a much smaller compass, thus enabling the student to get through with the whole work.

The bulk of a volume! This is an important consideration when speaking of framing a new course of studies. We distrust huge college books, and would rather select a little 12mo containing but few principles– provided they are well chosen and clearly enunciated– than a large 8 vo, crowded with facts, and exhibiting the whole doctrine in an indigestible manner. We have so little time to devote to the mutifarious sciences which necessarily compose our curriculum!

We are in favor, however, of very large print. Dugald Stewart's Elements, as printed at the Cambridge Press, are certainly easier to understand than the diamond edition to be found in most libraries.

The first part of the above work, we select; not without the deep regret of being unable to find time for the study of the second. This volume was written, taught and studied, twenty years before the second part issued from the author's pen; and it may be considered as an independent work. Our admiration for Dugald Stewart is unbounded; and we do not hesitate to say that his Elements, together with a compact manual of the History of Philosophy, is sufficient to impart to the student a faithful, though elementary, conception of the science.*

---

* Tennemann's Manual is excellent, but Johnson's Translation is so inferior, and our prejudices against Mr. Morell, who revised the latter, so insuperable, that we give the preference to a French compendium by Charmat.

It is in this Department, that we expect the greatest efforts on the part both of the student and his instructor. Lectures, and elucidations derived from practical illustrations, free from cant and, if possible, technical phraseology; a constant watch over the audience to detect what is understood and what is not so; questions plainly stated, –with some instructors it is more difficult to comprehend the question than give the answer–; repeated generalization of the substance in new language every time, &c – must often be resorted to, if the instructor has truly in view the mental improvement of his pupils,– for indeed, Philosophy, "the thinking of thought, the recoil of mind upon itself, is the most improving of mental exercises, conducing above all others to evolve the highest and rarest of the intellectual powers." †

---

† Edinb. Rev. Apr. 1849.

DEPARTMENT OF CHEMISTRY, GEOLOGY AND MINERALOGY

6. The utility and invigorating qualities of these studies are too obvious to require any vindication whatever. At this very moment,

there is scarcely a North Carolinian who does not feel the necessity of the science of Geology. The Dan and Deep River coal fields, the iron ore of Nash, and the Guilford copper mines, point out the future destinies of the Old North State; and farmers, lawyers and merchants are seen daily to quit the plow, the brief and the yardstick, to go in search of these bountiful gifts of Nature. Nor will they seek in vain! And if their energetic endeavors sometimes create a smile of incredulity, let it not be forgotten that Science has not yet uttered its last words nor Experience belied the promise of its adepts.

In this Department, Botany, Zoology and Physiology are studies in the Sophomore year.

Chemistry occupies two recitations a week throughout the Junior year. The course is that followed everywhere. Beginning with the history and nomenclature, the student is carried through the Laws of Heat, Light, Electricity &c &c., to Pneumatic and Organic Chemistry, embracing the Acids, metals &c. and illustrating the doctrine of chemical reaction, the Atomic Theory &c by numerous experiments, in the preparation of which the students are called upon to assist, so as to become familiar with chemical manipulations. They also have frequent exercises on the blackboard in chemical problems, solved by formulae and calculation.

In the Senior class, they study Mineralogy and Geology. It is useless to add that the great mineral zones are described by references to maps and sections; and in the lectures the appropriate minerals and specimens are often exhibited and noticed with reference to the geological formations of the State, and to the relations of all their features to the agriculture and other resources of the country.

DEPARTMENT OF DRAWING, PAINTING AND PENMANSHIP.

7. The number of recitations in this Department is rather large, but we must bear in mind that it is taken from days hitherto devoted to idleness or pleasure. Drawing may be easily rendered a good relaxation of the mind and a source of enjoyment to students. It will besides endow them with a talent both useful and agreeable.

In this Department, one hour every Monday morning is devoted to Penmanship, and one also on Saturday morning, to Geographical maps.

In the Sophomore year, they practice the rudiments of drawing, shades and ornament.

In the Junior, Figure, Perspective and Landscape.

In the Senior, Drawing as applicable to the Mechanical Arts and Architecture and Painting in water colors.

DEPARTMENT OF GYMNASTICS.

8. It cannot be doubted that the generality of our students do not present that healthy appearance so often to be found in the gymnasia

of Wurtemberg or High School of England. This physical defect may be ascribed to several causes. viz: the quantity and quality of the food which they so rapidly eat three times a day without the use of tonics of any kind; the immoderate use of tobacco, and the total want of exercise.

No one can reasonably expect to reform all these evils at once. Meat, American students must have often and plentifully; tobacco, they will chew and smoke; wine might be dangerous; but exercise can be easily enforced on them.

We scarcely see the inmates of our colleges ride, fence, row or take long walks. Many of them are fond of hunting, but few indulge in the sport. In fact, the greatest part of the leisure time alloted [sic] to them, they spend in loitering from room to room, or lolling on their beds to puff bad cigars and doze over trashy novels. Yet, who can deny the absolute necessity of bodily exercise? The ancients, who had better views in many respects than the moderns in the art of training youth, made of gymnastics one of the four requisites of their education. The Greeks and the Romans were thoroughly convinced that the mind could not be sound, unless the body was likewise in a healthy state. Hence it is that we never clear away the rubbish of any Hellenic city, without discovering the ruins of several palaestrae. There is hardly a single ancient author on medicine who does not explicitly state that gymnastics are as necessary for the preservation of health as drugs for the cure of disease. We even hear of a celebrated adept in the art of healing (Asclepiades), who was so ingenious in the invention of exercise, to supply the place of physic, that by these means– to use the words of Pliny– "he rendered himself the delight of mankind."

If gymnastics, then were considered by such physicians as Hippocrates and Galen, as so conducive to the health of men who passed nearly their whole existence in public squares, how necessary must we deem bodily exercise when thinking of youths who are unavoidably subjected during many hours to immobility and confinement? We therefore earnestly urge the introduction at all schools, academies and colleges, of jumping, climbing, wrestling, boxing, running, &c; in fine, of compulsory exercise of any kind. This, they must have, were it only, like Petarius, at the end of every second hour, a twirling of their chairs for five minutes;– but as the latter might create confusion in the classroom, we have instead, a gymnasium in the open air, in the practice of which all the students are required to partake during one hour every day except Saturday and Sunday, from 12 to 1 P. M., under the supervision of an instructor who also fills the office of marshal.

As College Marshal, he is charged with the general superintendance [sic] of all the buildings, grounds, &c. He oversees all repairs and cleansings which the Faculty may direct; informs the Professors of any disturbance caused by the students, and assists in detecting the offenders. He has also the supervision of the servants employed about the College, hires them, receives and measures the wood; and no bill for fuel can be paid without his certificate.*

---

* There are in New York and Philadelphia, many German "turners" who are qualified for the office, and whose services could be secured at a salary of $400 per annum.

EXPENSES AND BUILDING ACCOMODATIONS [sic]

VI. But very few colleges in America can support themselves without the help of private donations or appropriations from the Legislature. The University of Virginia, Brown, Alabama and many others, if not all, were liberally endowed even before they went into operation; and the South Carolina College has cost the State nearly a million of dollars within the last 45 years. Hence it is that these Institutions can afford so to lower their price of tuition as to render it accessible to all. At the University of Michigan, they make no charges whatever; at Bowdoin, they amount only to $24, at Hamilton, $26, Dartmouth $27; but these colleges have resources of their own; and as our Institution is supposed to rely solely upon itself for support, we adopt the average price for tuition, room rent, &c, &c, viz $60 per annum.

The number of students is limited to 200, which yields an income (on paper) of $12,000. This sum we deem sufficient to cover the actual expenses of the Institution.

For the present, and with the understanding that they will be doubled as soon as the endowment will allow it, we fix the President's
   salary at $1,500
   the Professor's at   1,200
   the adjunct Professor's at   1,000
   the Marshal's at   500

We think it impossible to get and keep men of abilities for less than 2 or $3,000 a year, inasmuch as their labors are great and confinement still greater. Nor must we lose sight of the fact that we require from our instructors accomplishments and talents not often to be found in the generality of American Professors. It is a misconceived economy or near-sighted policy, to curtail the teacher's compensation. It tends to render him anxious to leave the college as soon as he can obtain a more profitable situation elsewhere; and thereby hinders him from bringing to the discharge of his duty, the predilection, nay, the enthusiasm, so necessary to the prosperity of any literary Institution.

As for the building accomodations [sic], they consist of 100 dormitories,– 6 recitation rooms, one of which serves for a Laboratory; 10 studying rooms for 15 students, each containing desks and a rostrum;– 2 debating Halls for 100 members; a Library, which is also to be used for the drawing classes and a Chapel. The whole comprehended in one building, 3 stories high – fronting 210 feet, with wings of 100 x 40 feet each, and a portico on the main building of 40 feet front and 10 feet projection; a corresponding projection to be in the rear of the building, viz:

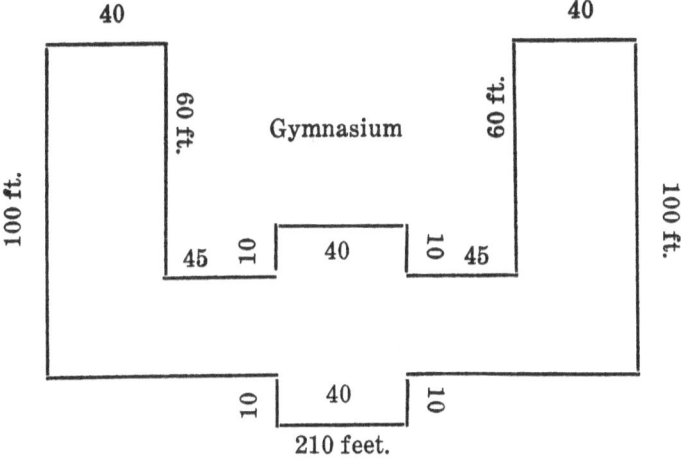

"WHETHER THE STUDENTS SHOULD STUDY IN PRIVATE OR CLASSROOMS?"

VII. It is the collegian's nature to be prone to idleness; to consider study as a severe infliction and the college discipline as a tyranny, which he constantly and ingeniously strives to elude. Even those who are urged to application by the laudable ambition of acquiring knowledge, college honors or the commendations of their fond parents, often look upon the day's recitation as a task which they endeavor to alleviate. Hence their frequent use of translations, readiness to avail themselves of the Professor's occasional mistakes in giving out the lesson; and those little associations when the preparation of the lesson is carried out in concert, each member contributing his share of lexical researches to the mass; or the best scholar in the company translating the text aloud for the accomodation [sic] of his artful classmates.

This natural tendency to self-indulgence is greatly abetted by the excessive liberty granted to our students. Provided they are in their rooms at a stated time, nothing more seems to be required of them. They may occupy the study hours in reading newspapers, dozing in a rocking chair or whittling soft pine sticks, no one will or can compel them to study. If they do not know their lesson, they get a bad mark, and in the opinion of the Faculty, stand low in the scale of scholarship. A very unenviable estimation, no doubt, but which has no influence whatever upon their ulterior conduct. They are too well aware that a student is hardly ever dismissed from college on account of deficiency; or refused to be re-instated after an easy trial, when perchance he has been "disapproved." In some institutions it may even be said that the greatest danger he runs of losing his diploma is to be short of the money required to pay the college fees.

Such an unlimited freedom of action is altogether out of place within the walls of a college. Both the curriculum and the study must be compulsory and attended to. No door should be left open to shifting or evasions of any kind. Every expedient should be adopted to obtain the utmost degree of perseverance and continued attention; in fine, all inducements, all temptations towards inaction and idleness must by all means be removed. Close application, prolonged mental efforts should be enforced on students, whatever be their age, wealth, intellectual superiority or family connections. Is there anything more unjustifiable, more revolting, than to see a student placed above the rules of college, and setting at defiance both teachers and citizens, because he is the son of an influential man?

We repeat it: the spirit of competition or the hope of reward stimulates only a few; necessity works upon all. Young men naturally shrink from protracted and active thinking, but we firmly believe with Sir William Hamilton, that mental exertions, however difficult and irksome when first enforced on the student, after a while become easy and agreeable. "This effort," says the great Scotch metaphysician, "is at first and for a time painful, positively painful, in proportion as it is intense, and comparatively painful, as it abstracts from other and pleasurable activities. It is painful because its energy is imperfect, difficult, forced. But, as the effort is gradually perfected, gradually facilitated, it becomes gradually pleasing; and when finally perfected, that is, when the power is fully developed, and the effort changed into a spontaneity, becomes an exertion absolutely easy, it remains purely, intensely and alone insatiably pleasurable." *

---

* Discuss. "Oxford as it might be." 693.

Every class, except the Senior, is divided into four equal sections. Each one of these sections studies apart; thus forming little agglomerations of twelve students, more or less, who study in common, in a room separate from the rest, and under the responsible supervision of a Senior who prepares at the same time his own recitations. This Monitor who is taken from among the most respected and orderly in his class, is exempted from paying college fees of any kind; and, if necessary, is sworn to a faithful discharge of his monitorial duties. Like the sargeant at the Polytechnic School, or the *Obergeselle* at the Gymnasium of Pforta, he is responsible for whatever disorder occurs in the classroom; he reports the students who appear to muse, talk or remain idle instead of studying, and aids his companions in the preparation of their lessons, either in answering questions or repeating occasionally the Professor's recommendations.

Each member of the Faculty visits in turn all the class-rooms during study hours.

The hours of recitation are for the first divisions of all classes, twenty minutes before Seven, and twenty minutes to Eleven A.M. and Four P.M.

The second divisions recite at Eight A.M., Two P.M., and twenty minutes past Five P.M. (as soon as the endowment will allow an increase of instructors, the different divisions of the four classes will all recite and study at the same hour.)

Two hours are allotted for the preparation of each lesson; the first of which they study in their own dormitories, at night; the second and the third, in their respective classrooms, in the manner above stated, and during the two hours preceding recitation.

At the ringing of the bell, they march out to the Recitation-room under the conduct of the monitors. The Professor awaits the class at the door; makes his entrance after the former has called the roll and repaired to his own recitation room; the whole class rise as he enters, and the recitation commences. It takes one hour and twenty minutes; these twenty minutes being devoted to a verbal exposition of the next lesson, and whatever remarks the Professor may deem necessary to elucidate the text-books; he then dismisses the class. Like the former public Reader at Oxford, he is required to remain for a certain time in the room after the lesson is over, in order to answer all pertinent questions that the monitors cannot explain, and which might be put to him by the students.

The Seniors study all their lessons in private; but recite in the same manner as the other classes.

The balance of the time is altogether at the student's disposal.

"WHETHER STUDENTS SHOULD BOARD AT PRIVATE HOUSES OR AT A STEWARD'S HALL?"

VIII. Experience has shown that it is impossible for a college of any importance to establish a Steward's Hall which can give permanent satisfaction to students, the faculty and parents. Most of the rebellions that formerly occurred in our literary institutions arose from the scantiness or inferior quality of the fare served up at the college tables. Even in Europe, where the students are certainly not too prone to sedition, when we hear of an academical rebellion, we may take it for granted that it has originated in the bad quality of the food; – which, indeed, is often intolerable.

At Harvard, from their first establishment in the year 1636, until 1849, when they were abolished, Commons have been an incessant source of disturbance, the trustees, worried by continual and just complaints, erected some years since a new hall, and greatly improved both the fare and accommodations. Six months had not yet elapsed under this arrangement, "before," says President Josiah Quincy,[50] "an open revolt of the students took place on account of the provisions, which it took more than a month to quell." * Not long ago in the South

* Quincy's Hist. Harv. Univ. Vol. 11. 540.

Carolina College, within the precincts of which a Steward's Hall had been lately built at great expense, and where the fare was both clean and plentiful, the dissatisfaction soon became so great, that it manifested itself by an open sedition. After dismissing eighty or ninety students, the Faculty were at last obliged to render Commons optional and to license private boarding houses.

If we could, as at Cambridge or Oxford, where the tables are constantly supplied with such an abundance of wholesome and well prepared victuals, flanked by decanters of beer, port and sherry, that no Cantabrigian, from the supercilious Fellow Commoner to the modest and diligent *Sizar* who dines gratis on the remains of his table, is ever heard to utter a complaint, we would recommend, perhaps, the introduction of commons; unfortunately all the college records testify against such expectations. The experiment of satisfying all parties on that score, has been repeatedly tried, and the more so because at one time it was thought indispensable to the welfare of the institution that students should take their meals in common, and under the supervision of the professors; but the result of such attempts has always been either a transient success or a total failure. The bursarship invariably falls into the hands of a steward who is either incapable of providing for a good table, or too eager to become rich at the expense of the students' comfort and appetite.

At Yale, whilst the overseers earnestly endeavored to conciliate the students in their efforts towards improving commons, "the conviction was increasing that they were no essential part of college," to use President Woolsey's own words, "that on the score of economy they could claim no advantage; that they degraded the manners of students and fomented disorder. The experiment of suppressing them has hitherto been a successful one." † We may add, that this example has

† Presid. Woolsey. Hist. Disc. 1850.

been followed by the majority of colleges, North and South; steward's halls and commons have been abolished, "and with them have departed the discords, dissatisfactions and open revolts of which they were so often the cause."

---

[50] Josiah Quincy (1772-1864), president of Harvard College (1829-1845), author of *A History of Harvard University*.

So as to avoid all such difficulties, and believing that it is not necessary to restrict the student's liberty in such paltry matters as eating, either in private or in common, nay, that the stir and bustle generally exhibited at the table is beneficial to their digestion and comfort, we allow our pupils to take their meals at private boarding houses, – provided the house is licensed by the Faculty; a lady always presides at the table; no intoxicating liquor is permitted to be drunk in the establishment, and the misconduct of students, at any time in the house, is reported to the Faculty.

"WHETHER THE INSTITUTION SHOULD BE DENOMINATIONAL OR OTHERWISE?"

IX. We confess to be altogether unable to find a single plausible reason in behalf of denominational colleges; on the other hand, we deem it obvious that any institution purporting the education of Christian youths, should be free from sectarian influence.

Religion must be imparted to collegians, not, indeed, to promote the interest or progress of any particular creed, but to supply the most imperious of human wants; purify and direct all the aspirations and passions of man, and fit him for the discharge of those solemn duties which he owes to himself, to God and the Commonwealth.

Let the Bible then be taught and expounded within the walls of our college; let its truths and sublime precepts in all their lofty simplicity be inculcated on the youthful mind of our pupils; let them even exalt in hymns of praise and gratitude for the precious gifts which the Supreme Ruler has so bountifully bestowed on them; but let us beware of dogmatic teachings, lest we should entail a continuance of religious intolerance, and weaken the cause of Protestantism in perpetuating the strife of sects.

Our institution, therefore is not denominational. Clergymen of different denominations, taken from among the Faculty and Ministers in the neighborhood, are invited to preach by turns to the students.

All the classes are required to attend Divine Worship in the College Chapel on Sunday forenoon; and in the afternoon the Freshmen and Sophomores recite in the Historical parts of the Old and New Testaments.

The Juniors, in Wayland's Moral Science and the Seniors in Butler's Analogy.

"OTHER THINGS NECESSARY TO BE KNOWN AND DETERMINED IN ESTABLISHING AND CONDUCTING AN INSTITUTION."

X. 1. It is only just that in departing from the institution after having fulfilled all his collegiate duties, the students should receive a certificate of proficiency. In point of reason, a few lines written by the President, in the name of the Faculty, on a mere scrap of paper, would answer as well as the most elaborate parchment; but, at times, especially when dealing with young men, we must make the part of human frailty. A diploma, nay, a title, is then necessary.

In itself, the word *"Baccalaurens,"* (if really derived from *baccis laureis*,) may be properly affixed to a proficiency in sciences or belles-lettres, without requiring the bachelor to be at all versed in the humanities. The addition of the words *artium* or *literarum* to the title of bachelor, alone, on account of a long assimilation with a proficience in the Latin and Greek languages, might perhaps appear out of place if applied to our graduates. But, in using the term "Bachelor of Philosophy," we can give no just offence to the intractable votaries of Oxford, of Cambridge, of Yale; and will thus realize, we trust, one of the highest aspirations of American students.

2. The graduating class is arranged in four divisions. The first division consists of the two students who have obtained the highest marks throughout the course, in all the departments, except gymnastics and Drawing; – these being mechanical accomplishments, oftener the gift of nature than the result of study. The Faculty confers on one the First Honor, and on the other the Second Honor. The Honors are never divided between two or more individuals. We know that the difference between the candidates is rarely, if ever, so slight as not to admit of a distinction; and, if in some institutions they are awarded to four, five and sometimes six students, this discrepancy must be ascribed generally to a catering for popularity or a tame apprehension of causing dissatisfaction to the class. Strange to say, in the South Carolina College, it was just the reverse, – an unlucky division of the First Honor between two scholars, brought about the change we now advocate.

The First Honor man delivers the Salutatory oration, and the Second Honor man, the Valedictory to the graduating class.

The second division consists of the six students who next to the Honor men stood the highest throughout the course in one or more departments. The best scholar in English or in Mathematics, for instance, receiving a separate distinction. This discrimination applies to all the Departments. The member of this division who stands the highest in the Department of Modern languages, declaims an original French oration at Commencement.

The third division consists of four second-rate students, taken from among those who distinguished themselves in the six above named departments.

The second and third divisions, (except the members who stood first only in gymnastics or drawing), deliver speeches on commencement day.

The last division is composed of the remaining Seniors who have simply passed their last examination.

3. The hope of a palpable reward, however slight in point of pecuniary worth, is at times a powerful incentive to students. The sets of finely bound books or the simple wreath of ivy awarded at the Sorbonne are often more highly valued than the most pompous newspaper accounts of these literary contests. It is a natural ambition which urges the student to untiring efforts, and it frequently achieves what all other means failed to accomplish. We feel confident that in many instances the "Deturs" of the Hopkin's Foundation,[51] have been more productive of good than the well-deserved commendations which the Professors rarely fail to lavish on their favorite pupils.

We therefore add to the diplomas of the First and Second Honor men, a set of not less than twelve books, finely bound; and to those who received the distinctions, six handsome volumes, all selected from standard authors. The distinction man in Drawing gets a box of Mathematical instruments; the best gymnastician receives a pair of silver spurs.

We also award for the best English Composition– the competitors to be Freshmen, – a gold medal. For the best historical dissertation – the competitors to be Sophomores – a gold medal. For the best French composition – the competitors to be Juniors, – a gold medal. For the best essay on Moral or Intellectual Philosophy – the competitors to be Seniors, – a gold medal.

4. The roll is not called in the Chapel; the monitors report the members of their sections who are absent. Each section has a separate pew. Calling the roll aloud, will do for a barrack, but it is not becoming in a place of public worship.

5. The use of tobacco, in any way, is strictly prohibited. The faculty may remove from the institution any student who has thrice infringed this rule.

6. Our college confers no honorary degrees of any kind; nor are the graduates of three years standing, or more, entitled to the "Mastership."[52]

7. No student can be admitted to a partial course; – all the studies being obligatory.

---

[51] Edward Hopkins was a London merchant who came to this country in 1637, was several times governor of Connecticut, and made some important educational gifts to New England for the purpose of providing "some encouragement in those foreign plantations, for the breeding up of hopeful youths, both at the grammar school and college, for the public service of the country at future times." Part of the income of one of his gifts is still used at Harvard College for the purchase of books called "Deturs" for meritorious students. Detur is the Latin for "Let there be given."

[52] Before 1860, and perhaps later, the master's degree was often conferred on graduates of three years beyond the A.B. degree, upon the payment of a fee, no additional work or attendance being required. Professor Samuel Eliot Morison says (Three Centuries of Harvard, p. 35) that "in the nineteenth century it was a saying that all a Harvard man had to do for his Master's degree was to pay five dollars and stay out of jail." For a good account of the practice of awarding honorary degrees in the United States see Stephen E. Epler, Honorary Degrees: A Survey of Their Use and Abuse (Washington, D. C.: American Council on Public Affairs, 1943).

CONCLUSION

No mercenary motive urged me to compose this essay. I was convinced that a thorough reform in our collegiate system was absolutely necessary to the progress and prosperity of our State; and in the hope that I might thus promote the welfare of North Carolina, I gladly availed myself of this opportunity of committing to writing the results of several years' observation and experience on the subject of collegiate education.

Whether the accompanying project will ever be carried out; and, if so, prove successful, is a question which time alone can solve. Suffice it to say, that I sincerely believe in its practicability; and to the stern critics who will not fail to censure the freedom of my remarks or carp at the boldness of the foregoing scheme, I can only answer, in the words of the eminent Doctor Thornwell,[53] that "in the effort to realize the conception of a perfect education, we are apt to forget that there is no such thing as absolute perfection in the matter, that all excellence is relative, and that the highest recommendation of any plan is that it is at once practicable and adjusted to the wants and conditions of those for whom it is provided." *

---

* Rev. Dr. Thornwell. Letter to Gov. Manning.

H. H.
State University. Aug. 10th 1855.

---

[53] The letter of President James H. Thornwell, of the South Carolina College, to Governor Manning of that state, on education, November, 1853, ranks high among the most important statements on that subject produced in the South prior to 1860. The General Assembly of South Carolina ordered the publication of 5,000 copies of the letter. In this letter Thornwell points approvingly to the report of Victor Cousin for which Harrisse apparently had high respect; and Thornwell's position that an educational institution should be non-denominational but not anti-Christian may have influenced Harrisse's views on this subject.

REPRINTED FROM
The North Carolina Historical Review

www.ingramcontent.com/pod-product-compliance
Lightning Source LLC
Chambersburg PA
CBHW031715230426
43668CB00006B/222